Un/Bound

Free Black Virginians, 1619–1865

Un/Bound

Free Black Virginians, 1619–1865

Essays by
Melvin Patrick Ely
Evanda S. Watts-Martinez
Sabrina G. Watson
Cassandra L. Newby-Alexander
Stephen Rockenbach

VMHC g

Virginia Museum of History & Culture
in association with D Giles Limited

First published jointly in 2025 by GILES
An imprint of D Giles Limited
66 High Street,
Lewes, BN7 1XG, UK
www.gilesltd.com

ISBN: 978-1-913875-61-9

For the Virginia Museum of History & Culture:
Editor: Graham Dozier, Manager of Publications & Scholarship
Images in this book from the collection of the Virginia Museum of History & Culture are credited as VMHC.

For D Giles Limited:
Copy-edited and proof-read by Jenny Wilson
Designed by Matt Wilson
Produced by GILES, an imprint of D Giles Limited
Printed and bound in Europe

EU GPSR authorised representative:
LOGOS EUROPE, 9 rue Nicolas Poussin, 17000,
La Rochelle, France
E-mail: contact@logoseurope.eu

Front and back cover, and pp. 18–19: "View of Richmond, Virginia" (detail), John W. Hill, 1847, watercolor. *VMHC*

Frontispiece: View of Liberty [Bedford] and the Peaks of Otter (detail), Edward Beyer, 1855, oil on canvas. *VMHC*

MIX
Paper | Supporting responsible forestry
FSC® C118234
FSC
www.fsc.org

Contents

Foreword

In 1860, as the United States was on the brink of civil war over the question of human chattel slavery, approximately 60,000 free Black people called Virginia home. In cities like Petersburg and in rural enclaves like Charles City and Prince Edward counties, they lived dynamic and varied lives, even as more than 500,000 of their Black neighbors were held in bondage under the abominable institution of slavery. Of all the slave states, only in Maryland did a greater population of free Black people reside. They were farmers and barbers, sailors and seamstresses, and husbands and wives. They attended church services, wrangled with their neighbors in court, and strove to educate their children. Their lives were rich and full, and yet their stories remain largely untold in the traditional rendering of Virginia's history. Their stories must no longer be ignored or erased.

That's why the three of us, former members of the Virginia Board of Education, undertook an effort to tell a more complete history of Virginia's pre–Civil War Black population through an unprecedented collaboration with representatives from five Virginia institutions of higher education (Norfolk State University, Virginia State University, the College of William & Mary, Longwood University, and Richard Bland College) and the Virginia Museum of History & Culture.

We had several goals: to create this publication and an exhibition entitled *Un/Bound: Free Black Virginians, 1619–1865*; to better share the rich history of Virginia's pre–Civil War Black population, including the accomplishments made by free Blacks in spite of oppression; to educate audiences about the multifaceted narratives of Black Virginians, including those who lived, to some extent, outside the heinous bonds of chattel slavery; and to enable students and citizens to fully appreciate the significance of this "untold story" at a time when there is much discussion about history and its importance in our ever-changing global existence.

For decades, scholars like those featured in this publication made great strides in educating readers about enslaved Black Virginians. The centrality of slavery to Virginia's history is obvious, but it is not the whole story. Neglecting

Freemen of Color, Richmond, Virginia, William Abbott Pratt, ca. 1850, hand-colored quarter plate daguerreotype.

Chrysler Museum of Art purchase with funds given by Christina and Dr. George M. Kemp, and in memory of Alice R. and Sol B. Frank to study the lives of Virginians who were not enslaved prior to emancipation is a missed opportunity to explore an under-told and often times inspirational story about our Commonwealth's past. *Un/Bound*—both the book and the exhibition—fills a critical gap in the public's understanding of these courageous and captivating people.

What did it mean to be free and Black in a slave state like Virginia? How did these people—unbound by slavery but nevertheless oppressed because of the color of their skin—impact and shape our Commonwealth? References to free Black Virginians exist throughout our state's history, beginning with early English colonization through the close of the Civil War. Descendants of those who were free before emancipation keep their ancestors' legacies alive to this day through oral tradition, genealogical research, and preservation of artifacts passed down over generations. By delving into collections across the Commonwealth, whether the authoritative records of the state or testimonies left by free Black people themselves, we can better understand how Virginia's legal, economic, and social systems evolved and operated, and how freedom to people of African descent did not guarantee equality. Studying their choices, actions, and interior worlds allows us to ask important questions about the meaning of freedom and who enjoys its privileges, while we honor them and their courageous lives.

The free Black people you will encounter in *Un/Bound* lived in a society that equated black skin with slavery. Not enslaved but by no means full citizens, free Black Virginians persevered in a liminal state. They faced significant challenges and injustices. But their experiences also show us that free Black Virginians often built lives of pride and achievement, despite being surrounded by the inhumanity of slavery and racial oppression.

One cannot appreciate the achievements of free Black Virginians without comprehending the magnitude of the challenges they faced. The people in *Un/Bound* uplift and instruct through their successes achieved on their own terms while navigating within societies defined and diminished by white supremacy.

In this book, you will encounter people in the Commonwealth who purchased their freedom and built their fortunes in the mid-1600s, just as the Virginia General Assembly was codifying laws explicitly defining the terms of racialized slavery; Reverend Moses, a free itinerant preacher who risked his life to build a site of worship for free and enslaved Virginians outside of Williamsburg in the 1770s; and Esther Evans, manumitted in Accomack County in 1806. That same year the Virginia General Assembly enacted legislation requiring that all emancipated free persons vacate the state within a year of gaining their freedom. In 1851, although Evans was ordered to appear in court for remaining in Virginia for forty-four years after she was required by law to leave, she ignored her court date. You will learn the significance of her refusal to appear.

Seeking a sense of freedom they were denied at home, many free Black Virginians sailed for the African colony of Liberia beginning in the 1820s. Others left Virginia because they felt a calling to spread the Gospel, and some traveled to West Africa to expand their business ventures. You will learn about Joseph Jenkins Roberts and his family who, in March 1829, boarded the *Harriet* and braved the Atlantic to pursue opportunities not afforded them in Virginia. Though moderately successful in Virginia, Roberts became head of state in the fledging republic that hugged Africa's Atlantic coast.

In *Un/Bound* you will also meet Alfred W. Harris and James Major Colson, Jr., two men born free before the Civil War, who became leaders in post-emancipation Virginia. Their accomplishments and the obstacles they confronted show us what was both possible and impossible for free Black Virginians during the Reconstruction era and beyond.

Uncovering the "untold stories" allows us to better understand the complete history of our Commonwealth and our country. Understanding the history of free Black Virginians permits us to more fully comprehend the long and arduous struggle for freedom, equality, and democracy that we as Americans have been engaged in for more than 400 years.

We are grateful to the Virginia Museum of History & Culture for helping bring *Un/Bound* to life in this publication and exhibition.

James W. Dyke, Jr.
Former Virginia Secretary of Education

Tim Sullivan
President Emeritus, College of William & Mary

Alvin J. Schexnider
Former Interim President, Norfolk State University

Acknowledgments

Un/Bound: Free Black Virginians, 1619–1865—both the exhibition and this companion publication—were made possible by the dedication and generosity of many individuals and organizations. *Un/Bound*, the exhibition, was presented by The Commonwealth of Virginia and Google Data Centers. The exhibition also received generous supporting sponsorship from Melanie Trent De Schutter, Dr. Tamara Charity-Brown & Carlos M. Brown, Conrad M. Hall, Dominion Energy, Huntington Ingalls Industries, McGuireWoods LLP, PNC Foundation, Riverside Health System, and Sentara Health. Additional support was also provided by Carilion Clinic, the Lettie Pate Evans Changing Exhibition Fund, Mr. & Mrs. W. Heywood Fralin, National Counseling Group, Thompson Hospitality, Washington Gas, and Balfour Beatty. The companion publication was made possible with generous support from *The Conrad M. Hall Endowment for the Study of Virginia History*.

The multi-year project that produced *Un/Bound*, the exhibition and this publication, benefited greatly from feedback provided by an engaged group of stakeholders, including descendants, teachers, museum colleagues, and community organization leaders. A very special thanks is due to James W. Dyke, Jr., former Virginia Secretary of Education; Tim Sullivan, President Emeritus, the College of William & Mary; and Alvin J. Schexnider, former Interim President of Norfolk State University—all passionate advocates for history and education—for their tireless support and for providing the genesis of this project. Our sincere thanks also go to these individuals and groups for their guidance: Kevin Brown and Diana Durham; Jillian Columbus, Owner, Explorers Studio LLC; Angela Davidson, Grants Administrator, Jim Stribling, volunteer, and Karen Hughes White, Director, Afro-American Historical Association of Fauquier County; Cassandra Good, Assistant Professor, Marymount University; Judith Ledbetter and Nancy Phaup, Richard M. Bowman Center for Local History; the Madden Family; Christine Mertens, Ph.D. Candidate, Leiden University and Roosevelt Institute for American Studies; Tonia Merideth, Oral Historian, Bray School Lab, the College of William & Mary; colleagues at the Library of Virginia, in particular, Lydia Neuroth, Project Manager for *Virginia*

Untold; Brian Palmer; the Quander family; and Dr. Gaila Sims, Curator of African American History, Fredericksburg Area Museum.

Exceptional scholars provided invaluable assistance with content development, in addition to writing the essays for this publication. We are deeply indebted to the following for their time and expertise: Dr. Melvin Patrick Ely, William R. Kenan, Jr. Professor of Humanities and Professor of History at the College of William & Mary; Dr. Cassandra L. Newby-Alexander, Professor of History and Endowed Professor of Virginia Black History and Culture and emeritus director of the Joseph Jenkins Roberts Center for African Diaspora Studies at Norfolk State University; Dr. Stephen Rockenbach, Professor of History, Interim Chair, Department of Sociology and Criminal Justice, and Assistant Dean of CHSS for Student Affairs, Virginia State University; Sabrina G. Watson, instructor and doctoral candidate, Department of History and Philosophy, Virginia State University; and Dr. Evanda S. Watts-Martinez, Director of Counseling Services, Assistant Professor of Education, and Co-Chair, Racial Justice & Equity Task Force, Richard Bland College of William & Mary.

Un/Bound was a collaborative effort by many talented staff at the Virginia Museum of History & Culture (VMHC). First, we wish to thank Dr. Elizabeth M. Klaczynski, Associate Curator, for championing this exhibition. Also, Heather Beattie, Collections Manager; Ajana Bradshaw, Exhibitions Coordinator; Bryan Condra, Exhibit Designer; Maggie Creech, Director of Education; Danni Flakes, Photographer; Sam Florer, Manager of Public Programs; Dr. James Herrera-Brookes, Melanie Trent De Schutter Sr. Director of Research & Publications; Dale Kostelny, Manager of Exhibition Production; Dr. Jan Meck, volunteer and researcher; Kathryn Potts, Curatorial Affairs Intern; Joseph S. H. Rogers, Pamela K. Royall Director of Partnerships & Community Engagement; Rebecca Rose, Sr. Director of Collections Management; Stacy Rusch, Senior Conservator; Adam Scher, Lisa & Bill Moore Vice President for Collections, Exhibitions, & Research; Christina Smith, Collections Management Assistant; and Andy Talkov, Sr. Director of Curatorial Affairs.

Finally, I wish to express my gratitude to all who generously support the Virginia Museum of History & Culture and empower its timeless work to save and share the history of Virginia.

Jamie O. Bosket

President & CEO, Virginia Museum of History & Culture

Introduction

What does freedom mean? This question cuts to the paradox at the heart of the American experience. We must remember that over the course of our nation's history not everyone has been granted the guarantee of universal equality.

American chattel slavery was explicit in its connection between race and bondage. White citizens lived without fear of enslavement. In fact, the stature of white people in the American South literally depended on there being a laboring, enslaved population composed of people of African descent. The 1619 arrival of the first "twenty and odd" Africans in the Colony of Virginia and the 1662 act passed by the General Assembly dictating that the children of an enslaved mother, no matter the father, would be born enslaved, set precedents for the entire North American continent. Slavery became institutionalized across the British colonies, particularly in the South; and colonies that once had operated with slavery as an important part of their economies became states in which the institution shaped and permeated every aspect of life. Societies with slavery became slave societies.

People enslaved in Virginia were of African descent, and yet not every Black person in Virginia was enslaved. As many as 60,000 free Black people lived in the Commonwealth before the Civil War (1861–65). The popular imagining of colonial North America and the antebellum American South equates blackness with slavery and whiteness with freedom. This is broadly correct. Many white Americans, particularly in the South, believed that free Black Americans could not and should not live freely and equally in the United States, despite the successes that their free Black neighbors achieved.

Un/Bound: Free Black Virginians, 1619–1865, an exhibition by the Virginia Museum of History & Culture, poses two important questions: first, who were these Virginians who were both free and Black, and what were their lives like? Here, we strove to depict Virginia's free Black community as it existed for more than two centuries. Community conversations and archival research spotlit new and neglected stories that reveal the lives of free Black people across public realms and private spaces throughout the Commonwealth. A common thread through the long arc of the history of free Black Virginians was the sheer volume of paper records—largely generated by state and local government—that framed free Black life from 1619 to 1865 and continues to shape our understanding of their lives in the present. Even as the exhibition seeks to present the totality of free Black life, the result is nevertheless an incomplete picture, with so many more stories to be told. This book aims to further that crucial work.

Secondly, to what degree were free Black Virginians really free, unbound as they were by the institution of slavery yet bound within a society that perceived them as inherently inferior and unworthy of equality? Essential to this work was to contrast free Black lives with the lives of free white and enslaved Black neighbors, exploring the liminal status that free Blacks occupied; a status that they navigated with acute awareness and abundant caution. People who strove to claim and maintain legal, economic, and personal liberty survived and succeeded in the shadow of slavery and in spite of unceasing prejudice.

Even though the 13th Amendment to the U.S. Constitution abolished slavery in 1865, and all Black Virginians became free, tracing the role that those already free in the antebellum period would play during the Reconstruction era (1865–77) demonstrates that their shrewdness prepared them to lead in a new world transformed by civil war. Indeed, the value of tracing the impactful legacy of these people, whether at home in Virginia, in Ohio, or on the West African coast, does not end in the nineteenth century.

Even more, the exhibition's impact is defined largely by the efforts of descendant families to ensure that their free ancestors' legacies endure. Through the preservation of oral histories and family heirlooms passed down over generations, these individuals meaningfully link past with present and demonstrate the value of history to create a shared sense of personal identity.

Un/Bound explores more than two centuries of Black Virginia history. Several salient themes serve as anchor points to structure the exhibition and guide visitors. From the beginning, free Black Virginians relied heavily on family and community, which often included enslaved people. Churches, fraternal and benevolent organizations, and neighborhood networks underpinned these familial and community networks, and formed the cornerstones of free Black people's worlds. Economic independence, opportunities for work and trade, and property ownership were aspirations that these Virginians strove for and achieved with varying degrees of success. At the same time, all these elements—the foundations of free Black life—were constantly influenced and shaped by a repressive statewide legal system.

The Virginia legal system made the lives of free Blacks unreasonably complex. Through consistent pressure, the state—from local courts to the Commonwealth's legislature—dehumanized free Black people and relegated them to second-class status. Through individual and communal actions, these Virginians navigated, resisted, and fled a state committed to denying them the rights that white Americans enjoyed, to better themselves, their families, and their communities.

The essays in this book, written by leading and emerging Virginia-based scholars of free Black history, are an important companion to the exhibition. They represent an opportunity to demystify and tell more stories of this important group—the challenges they faced and the contributions they made—to a broader audience. To provide continuity, each essay resonates with a theme or topic in the exhibition. They provide insight into the experiences of a significant population that is often rendered peripheral in most renderings of the sweep of Virginia history. Like the exhibition, the work of these scholars is an effort to make our shared past richer, more accurate, and meaningful to all.

Melvin Patrick Ely provides a comprehensive overview of the history of free Black Virginians in the book's opening essay. Beginning in the seventeenth century and concluding with the Civil War, Ely offers a nuanced interpretation of how free Black people navigated the intricacies of Virginia's racial hierarchy. Ely provides a window into multiple aspects of free Black life. Even as the essay emphasizes the importance of disseminating historical accounts that center Black experiences, he stresses the centrality of the power that white Virginians held over the lives of free Black people. Free Black people inhabited a society that was structured by and served white supremacy; their greatest successes came from recognizing and exploiting any cracks they could find.

Evanda S. Watts-Martinez sheds light on the religious lives of free Black Virginians in the early republic (ca. 1780–1830). Watts-Martinez outlines how Protestant faith traditions that evolved from the seventeenth century onwards helped shape Black identity, contributed to a sense of resilience in Black communities, and inspired acts of resistance against racial oppression and prejudice. Free Black Virginians developed and held fast to religious beliefs that defied an interpretation of Christianity that deemed slavery the natural status for Black people. These beliefs sustained them through both spiritual and earthly hardships, and affirmed that their quest for a fuller freedom was legitimate. Watts-Martinez outlines how the religious convictions of free Black Virginians also inspired the creation of underground religious sites and formal churches. These places served as the bedrock of communities and inspired free Black people's determination to pursue liberty, equality, and justice.

Sabrina G. Watson explores a resistance tactic that free Black Virginians employed in nineteenth-century Virginia. In 1806, the state's General Assembly passed what is commonly known as the "expulsion law." This act was replete with repressive provisions, with one of the most consequential being that any emancipated Black person who remained in the Commonwealth for more than twelve months after achieving freedom would forfeit their liberties and could be apprehended by county or corporation officials and forced into laboring for the benefit of those entities. It essentially constituted the threat of re-enslavement. However, the law was spottily enforced, demonstrating the limits of white power and the state more broadly. As a case study, we learn of individuals freed in Accomack and Isle of Wight counties who remained in the state well after the government required them to leave. Their quiet disregard for the law and the various summonses they received to appear in court represent officials' inability to control the free Black population in an absolute manner. Free Black Virginians, Watson demonstrates, displayed power through rejecting mandates requiring their removal from their home state.

Cassandra L. Newby-Alexander explores the opportunities offered and challenges posed to free Black people with the creation of the West African colony of Liberia in 1822. By exploring the varied motivations of those who emigrated to Liberia and by following in their footsteps, we can see how the colonization project, which became an independent nation unto itself in 1847, embodied many of the issues and contradictions that free Black Virginians faced at home. Originally conceived of by white elites who founded the American Colonization Society in 1816, Liberia was pictured as a distant land for an apparently troublesome and potentially dangerous free Black population that white people could not imagine living peacefully within society at large. But it was also a refuge that Black Americans used to escape white discrimination and violence, an opportunity to spread Christianity, and a new, bustling marketplace that free Black Virginians used to expand their fortunes. Newby-Alexander positions Joseph Jenkins Roberts, a free Black man born in Petersburg who became Liberia's first president, as a conduit through which to explore these overlapping tensions.

Finally, Stephen Rockenbach explores how free Black people took advantage of a new Virginia following emancipation in 1865. Rockenbach explains that Reconstruction initially brought newfound political power to Black Virginians who had been free before the Civil War, many of whom enjoyed advantages in property and social status unavailable to those who had been enslaved before the war. However, as Reconstruction waned and Jim Crow discrimination emerged, Black Virginians of all prior stations faced a new iteration of white supremacy that grouped all Black people together in a political and social underclass. They resisted this degradation through political activism, community-building, and education, even as white supremacy persisted as a formidable and dogged foe for more than a century.

Taken together, these essays emphasize that the free Black experience before emancipation was not monolithic. There was no composite free Black Virginian. Instead, their lives, communities, aspirations, and obstacles were complex and multifaceted. But a common thread weaves together the themes of the exhibition and the essays in this book, and that is the fraught relationship between race and freedom in Virginia and the broader United States. The experiences of free Black Virginians allow us to interrogate the limits of liberty, even as we better appreciate and celebrate the ingenuity, perseverance, and successes of people who lived under the burden of those constraints. *Un/Bound* is an invitation to consider historic freedom and unfreedom, and who remains in such liminal spaces in our world today, and to think about and act upon what we can all do to extend liberty and justice as we strive for a better nation for all.

Elizabeth M. Klaczynski
Associate Curator
Virginia Museum of History & Culture

African American Woman with Flag, 1860s, ambrotype.
Division of Work and Industry, National Museum of American History, Smithsonian Institution

Chapter 1

Black Freedom in Slaveholding Virginia

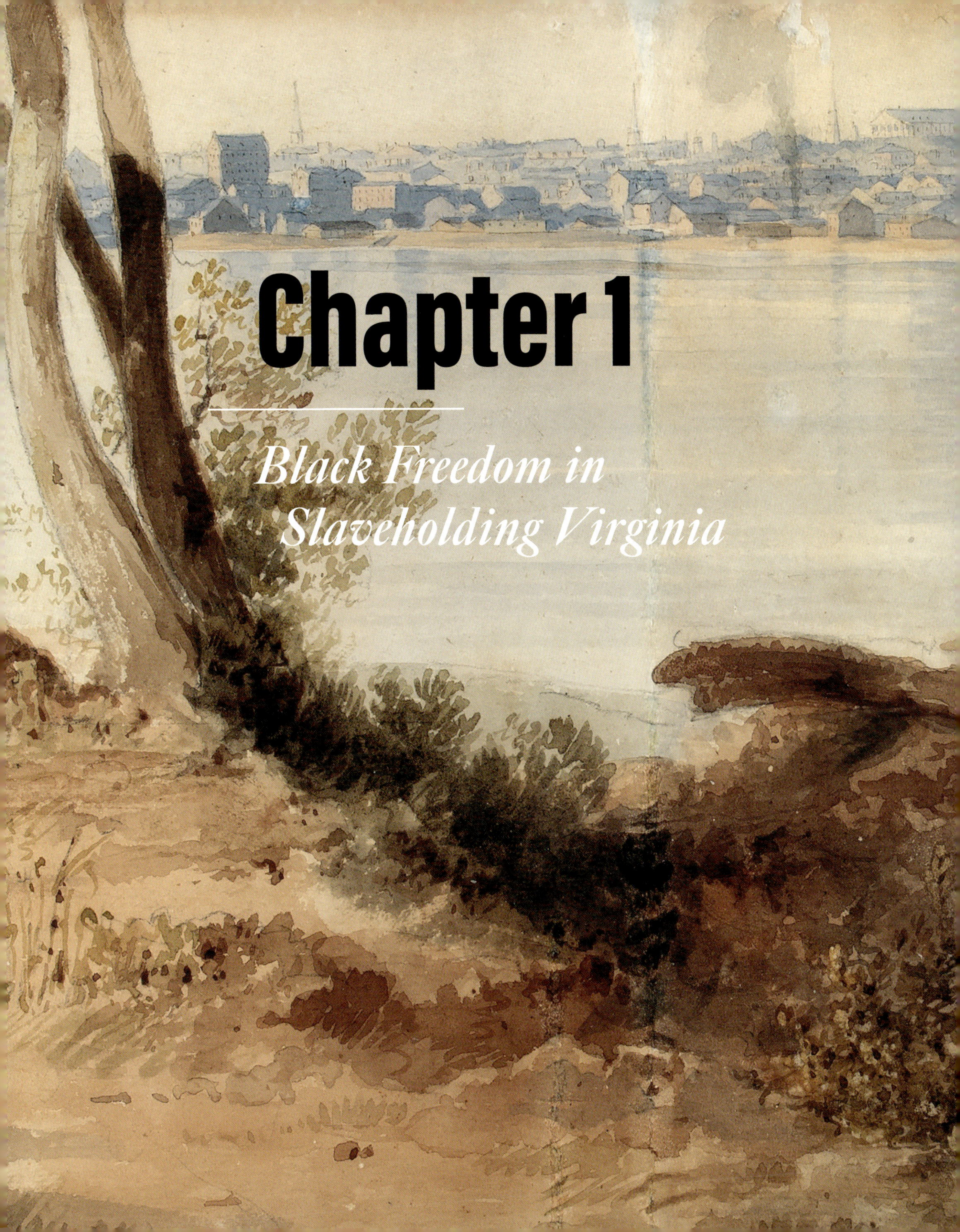

1

Black Freedom in Slaveholding Virginia

Melvin Patrick Ely

The history of free Black people in Virginia begins no later than the mid-1600s, though many would place the date earlier than that. The question of timing has been debated for many decades, often by people intent on making this or that polemical point. Many schoolchildren in Virginia are still taught that the first group of Africans who arrived in Virginia in 1619 were not slaves but rather indentured servants. Others point out that these people had been seized from a slave ship bound from Africa to the Americas and thus were already enslaved.

Everyone agrees that colonial Virginia's legal structures addressing slavery developed belatedly and gradually during the seventeenth century. But those laws were adopted to regulate a status—permanent bondage—that by the mid-1600s already applied de facto to most Black people in the colony. Crucially, this evolving legal code included laws adopted in the 1660s stating that conversion to Christianity did not alter one's enslaved status, and that any child of an enslaved woman was likewise enslaved for life. Similarly, children of a free mother shared her free status.

By the mid-seventeenth century, through extraordinary effort, some enslaved African and African American individuals managed to purchase their freedom. Others completed terms as indentured servants; a few converts to

Christianity even sued successfully for their liberty until that avenue was closed off by law. By 1668, nearly one-third of the Black people on Virginia's Eastern Shore had attained freedom. Free Black people bought land and occasionally even slaves or white indentured servants. They made use of the local courts, did business with whites, and otherwise conducted themselves much as white property owners did. Virginia's free Black population remained small—probably numbering a few hundred in the late seventeenth century.[1]

By the final years of that century, however, influential white Virginians sought to promote division between Black and white people of modest means. Those efforts, along with the importation of growing numbers of Africans, gradually caused the relative flexibility of earlier years to give way to a system that essentially equated Black skin with enslaved status. In 1705, Virginia's General Assembly adopted a comprehensive "act concerning servants and slaves." By then, indentured servitude was no longer an important element in the economy; enslaved Africans and African Americans constituted the colony's primary labor force. Virginia, formerly a *society with slaves*, was rapidly becoming a *slave society*.[2]

Occasionally, Virginia's legislature rewarded extraordinary service by enslaved individuals—for example, heroic rescues of imperiled people—by granting them freedom. And throughout the colonial period and beyond, there was cross-racial sexual contact. When white women bore children by Black fathers, those biracial children inherited their mothers' free status, although by law they were bound out to white people as apprentices until they reached adulthood (age thirty or thirty-one for both genders in colonial times, reduced to twenty-one for boys and eighteen for girls in 1774). From early on, then, the population this essay chronicles is most accurately referred to as *free people of color*—a designation that in the era of slavery was applied to almost all free people who had discernible African ancestry. For convenience, however, this discussion will echo the exhibition's use of the term "free Black people."[3]

In 1782, the General Assembly of now-independent Virginia adopted a law permitting slaveholders to freely manumit (set free) Black individuals—a practice that had been prohibited for most of the preceding century. That legislation almost immediately drew protests from some white people, but it also gave rise to actual manumissions in increasing numbers as the eighteenth century neared its end.[4]

By the early 1800s, some Virginia slaveholders had liberated large groups of Black people, most often through their wills. Robert Carter III of Nomony Hall plantation in Westmoreland County on the Northern Neck began gradually liberating his enslaved people in 1791; the process continued over many years, extending well beyond Carter's death and ultimately setting 500 to 600 Black people free.[5]

George Washington left a will freeing all the enslaved people he owned in his own right—well over 100 people—and directing that those under age 25 be taught to read and write. By 1810, Richard and Judith Randolph of Cumberland County had liberated more than ninety enslaved people and granted 350 acres of land to nine newly freed families.[6]

Manumitters such as these were typically motivated by Revolutionary or Christian ideals. Personal attachments also played a role in some cases; such affinities account for many small-scale manumissions, some affecting only one Black person. Manumissions for reasons of conscience, though enacted by only a small minority of slaveholders, explain why the free Black population of Virginia came to be much larger than was true in the cotton states. Those Deep South areas were settled after the wave of Revolutionary and evangelical unease over slavery had waned, and the few manumissions that did occur there were typically bestowed by slave owners only on their own biracial children.

In Virginia, too, some slaveholders manumitted children they had fathered with enslaved women, but other white men exploited and even sold their own children just as they would any other Black people they owned. Proposals to liberate all of Virginia's enslaved persons—even by "slow, sure, & imperceptable [*sic*] degrees," as Washington put it—won almost no support.[7]

Historians who set out to write African American history need to avoid the pitfall of producing instead histories of "race relations" that de-center the

Robert Carter III (1728–1804),
Thomas Hudson, 1753,
oil on canvas. *VMHC*

Black experience itself. Yet for nearly 250 years, Black Virginians lived in a system where white people exercised a monopoly over the political and judicial processes. Thus, the history of free Black people prominently includes the actions of whites, who followed up the manumission act of 1782 with laws designed to limit the freedom afforded to emancipated Black people.

Free Black Virginians could not vote or serve on juries. Virginia law forbade (or at least tried to forbid) Black people, enslaved or free, from gathering in groups larger than five in the daytime, or from coming together at all by night. Beginning in 1793, free Virginians of African descent were required to register with their local court, to carry with them a copy of that registration, and to renew it every three years (more frequently in cities). These "free papers" were at one and the same time an emblem of oppression, a symbol of freedom, and a practical safeguard against being apprehended as a fugitive from slavery. The tattered condition of registration papers that some free Black individuals turned in to local courts for one reason or another indicate that those people had carried their certificates on their person day-in and day-out. Requests for new papers from such people, or from those who had lost their documents, support that conclusion. Court clerks routinely provided duplicate documents, typically for a fee.[8]

The law provided that free Black people who were found to lack documentation of free status could be jailed until their free status was proven; they could then be hired out to involuntary servitude until they had earned back the costs of their incarceration. Especially in Richmond and perhaps in other places, this mechanism became both an engine of social control and a source of public revenue. The authors of the registration law had defined its purpose narrowly: to curb "the practice of [employers] hiring negroes and mulattoes, who pretend to be free, but are in fact slaves." Yet even a legitimately free Black person found to lack a copy of their registration could be arrested.[9]

Enforcement of this and many other oppressive laws varied considerably, however. In numerous places, monitoring seems to have been only occasional, and in general, efforts to restrict the movement of free Black Virginians from county to county, and from countryside to city, were ineffective. But even the possibility of enforcement, and its unpredictability, could create anxiety.

Two other laws typify the overall attitudes of white legislators toward free Black Virginians, the extent to which repressive measures were applied or not,

"View from Gambles Hill, Richmond, Va.," after Edward Beyer, 1857, tinted lithograph. *VMHC*

and the responses of the Black people at whom the laws were aimed. One of these laws in 1813–15 levied an annual head tax or "specific tax" of as much as $2.50 on free Black men. The head tax was reinstated in the 1850s at the rate of one dollar per year. The levy in the latter decade was insulting not only because it did not apply to white Virginians, but also because the funds it yielded were supposed to be used to fund the removal of free Black people from the state.[10]

Any Black person subject to this or any other tax who did not pay up was to be hired out by the authorities of his county or city to some white person in order to work off, at a very low daily rate, the amount of the unpaid tax. Some of the most striking documents found in nineteenth-century Virginia records relate to free Black non-payment of taxes. These include announcements that the sheriff on a given date would auction off the unfree labor of free Black tax delinquents. The bulletins were posted on the local courthouse door, and they included lists of all local free Black men who had not paid their taxes.

Some county documents list scores of Black tax insolvents; actually bidding them out would have required an effort of epic proportions. And in fact, other documents reveal that many sheriffs posted the annual announcement with no intention of rounding Black people up or conducting an auction of their labor. The state auditor recognized this reality, candidly advising one county sheriff to "go through all the forms" of hiring out but without following through. The sheriffs posted the lists because they were required to, and because they and their deputies received a monetary commission for each tax insolvent they listed. Free Black men in these counties came to understand that the tax-delinquent auctions were usually a legal fiction. Some did pay up, but many did not, staging a wordless tax revolt that generally drew no punishment.[11]

Another law, adopted by Virginia's General Assembly in 1806, provided that any Black person subsequently liberated must leave Virginia within one year or be subject to re-enslavement. This law has frequently been depicted as a response to the Haitian Revolution of the 1790s or to Gabriel's attempted slave rebellion around Richmond in 1800. Those events did have their effect, but the law of 1806 was passed some years after both and thus was not a direct response to either.

Rather, the law amounted to a compromise between two long-standing groups of white Virginians. One bloc opposed all manumissions. The other group rejected any restriction on would-be manumitters, a position they took either for altruistic reasons or to vindicate slaveholders' rights to deal with their human property as they saw fit. Few Black people were ever expelled under the law of 1806. A likely goal, and certainly the effect, of that law was to discourage manumissions without prohibiting them; a slaveholder who actually cared about the welfare of the enslaved might well hesitate to free them and thus subject them to the risk of expulsion from Virginia.

Even so, the free Black Virginian population grew very rapidly through 1830 and continued to rise steadily after that. This growth after 1800 occurred mostly through natural increase—the excess of births over deaths. By 1790, eight years after manumission was legalized, there were already nearly 13,000 free Black people in the state. That number grew to more than 30,000 by 1820, and to nearly 50,000 in 1840. By the eve of the Civil War, one in ten Black Virginians was free, and one in twenty free Virginians was Black.

Virginia's Black population, including its free component, lived primarily in the Piedmont and Tidewater regions. Fully half of the fifty counties in northwestern Virginia that would separate and form the new state of West Virginia during the Civil War had fewer than thirty free African American residents each in 1850; five had no free Black residents at all. Even in the area that remained part of Confederate Virginia, some mountainous counties had very few Black residents, free or enslaved. The white leaders who led the cleaving off of West Virginia hoped to keep the free Black population of their new state small; they promptly passed legislation aiming to prohibit entry of Black people, bond or free, into the state.

Still, there were eight slightly larger pockets of free Black settlement scattered around the central and northeastern parts of what would become West Virginia; in each of those counties, a couple hundred free people of color constituted one or two percent of the local population in the latter antebellum years. Something of an outlier in that part of the Commonwealth was Jefferson County on the Potomac River, site of Charles Town and Harpers Ferry; by 1850, more than 500 free Black people lived there—still a small fraction of the overall populace. Haywood (or Heyward) Shepherd, a free Black resident of Winchester who worked as a railroad baggage master in Harpers Ferry, was the first person killed by John Brown's party during Brown's attack on the federal arsenal in 1859.

In Piedmont and Tidewater Virginia, free Black populations varied considerably from locality to locality. In five counties, free Black people by 1850

View of Liberty [Bedford] and the Peaks of Otter (detail), Edward Beyer, 1855, oil on canvas. *VMHC*

"View of Harper's Ferry, Va. November 18th, 1863," B. Shunk, photograph. *Library of Congress*

represented a quarter of the entire free population and a similar fraction of the whole Black community or even more. Virginia's few cities contained very sizable free Black communities. Economic growth created job openings, which led free Black workers to migrate from rural areas. Many were drawn also to the vibrant Black social and cultural life of Petersburg, Richmond, and other larger centers.[12]

Some white people worried that free Black people would exert a subversive influence on the enslaved—and there was indeed a great deal of contact between the two Black groups. Some free Black people may have preferred, other things being equal, to marry other free persons of color. Yet love works its will, and, in a society where the overwhelming majority of Black people were enslaved, it was not unusual for free Black individuals to form spousal unions with enslaved persons. The term *spousal unions* applies because Virginia law did not recognize marriages in which either partner was enslaved.

A person whose husband or wife was owned by someone else faced the same peril that confronted enslaved couples—that the enslaved spouse might be sold or bequeathed to someone who lived far away. Tony White, a free Black man of Prince Edward County, managed to purchase his wife, Milly—but not before the couple's five still-enslaved children had been divided among three different white owners, one of whom moved to Missouri and took three of the Whites' children with him.[13]

Petersburg, Va., 1861–65, gelatin silver print photograph. *Library of Congress*

While some countered the threat of forcible separation by purchasing their spouse, many free Black people who did so decided not to formally liberate the spouse so as not to expose them to the possibility—however remote most of the time—of expulsion under the law of 1806. Most free Black individuals who appear in official records as slaveholders owned only one or two persons; these instances often represent the purely technical ownership of one's spouse or child.

But what would become of the formally enslaved partner at the death of the free Black spouse who legally owned him or her? Phil Bowman, a neighbor of Tony White, worked for a white man, William A. Allen; the two men appear together in some county tax rolls, suggesting that Bowman held a responsible position in the white man's business. Bowman and one of Allen's slaves, a woman named Priscy, became husband and wife. Then Allen suffered a financial meltdown; he had to surrender much of his property to satisfy creditors, and a local court ordered that Priscy Bowman be sold by the county sheriff. Phil Bowman attended that auction and succeeded in purchasing his wife with money lent him by the son of his current white employer.

Bowman now became one of the many free Black fictive slave owners who chose not to manumit his spouse. But then, in 1842, Phil died while Priscy was still very much alive; he provided for her by bequeathing her to James Venable, brother of the man who had helped him buy her, "for the purpose of her being taken care of." Bowman also left all his assets—a sizable fund of nearly $300—to support the widowed Priscy in "comfort." Venable carried out Phil Bowman's wishes faithfully—until Priscy Bowman lived so long that her maintenance fund apparently was exhausted. She spent the last two years of her life in the county poorhouse, where Venable seems to have placed her despite a law forbidding slaveholders to cast off enslaved people who were too old or too ill to be productive.

A second development following Phil Bowman's death shows that the distinction between free and enslaved Black people could sometimes undermine Black solidarity. Phil's free Black mother demanded that the money her son had left behind to cover Priscy's care be surrendered to her on the grounds that it was illegal to leave a bequest to an enslaved person. County officials diligently looked for a way to ensure that Priscy Bowman would continue to be provided for—and then Phil's mother involuntarily resolved the issue by dying.[14]

Carter G. Woodson, the father of African American history, uncovered an unsavory form that relationships between free and enslaved Black people occasionally took. Woodson reported that some free Black men purchased enslaved wives, "put them on probation for a few years," and then sold them "if they did not find them satisfactory." A few free Black Virginians owned enslaved people in numbers that suggest economic rather than familial motives. The federal census of 1830 shows William Daniel, a free Black man in Cumberland County in the center of the state, holding thirty-two people in bondage.[15]

A fundamental fact constraining free Black Virginian life was the conviction of many white Virginians that the emergence of a large free Black population would pose a burden if not a threat to themselves. St. George Tucker, one of the most persistent advocates of gradual emancipation in Virginia, was certain that "prejudice"—the racism and racial fears of most white people—would require any emancipation scheme to proceed with glacial slowness and to be accompanied by the departure of most liberated Black people to someplace other than Virginia.[16]

One way in which white people expressed this prejudice was through the defamations of Black character that some of them uttered and published. Even Tucker, who had declared that the races were created equal, believed that decades of oppression under slavery and continuing ostracism by whites might turn former slaves into "a numerous, starving, and enraged banditti" posing a threat to "the innocent descendants of their former oppressors." Others proclaimed that Black people born in freedom would lack "the habits of industry" their forebears had supposedly acquired under slavery, inevitably falling into "idleness, poverty, and dissipation" and becoming "a great pest" that burdened white society.[17]

Photograph of a Miniature of St. George Tucker (1752–1827), Charles Balthazar Julien Févret de Saint-Mémin, 1807, glass plate negative. *VMHC*

White Virginians frequently encountered industrious, upstanding Black people, yet they had long since imbibed racist attitudes that could override their own experience. The agronomist and proslavery extremist Edmund Ruffin noticed that many free Black men gravitated to river boating. These men poled "batteaux," each laden with five to seven tons of cargo, scores of miles up the winding rivers of Piedmont Virginia—yet Ruffin pontificated that Black men took up that job because of all occupations it was "the nearest to idleness."[18]

Tucker's assumption that most free Black people would need to depart from Virginia hints at the importance of the organized movement to resettle free Black people in Africa. Colonizationism was largely, though not entirely, a white response to the expansion of the free Black population after 1782. Some whites hoped that the promise of relocation would soften white opposition to the elimination of slavery through gradual emancipation. There were even colonizationists who believed that in Liberia formerly enslaved Black people could become "respectable members of the social compact, ornaments to science and the arts." But many other advocates of colonization saw their movement not as a means of promoting emancipation but rather as a device to get rid of those Black people who were already free. All the while, most free Black Virginians made it clear that they had no desire to leave their homes for a place they had never seen.[19]

White bias against free Black people sometimes led to dramatic outbursts of repression, but these were ultimately self-limiting because of indecision or outright dissension within the white community. The immediate reasons for some of these eruptions are now obscure. In 1816, the Prince Edward county court ordered that all residents of a nearby free Black settlement up to age twenty-one be bound out as apprentices. A document was drawn up listing everyone in that settlement by age; the binding-out order would have applied to seventy young people. But the order was never carried out; neither, apparently, was a similar measure aimed at twenty-four free Black children in 1829.[20]

In Accomack County on the Eastern Shore, free Black people long made up a larger fraction of the population than in any other county in the state. There, the overseers of the poor—an organ of local government—decided in 1825 to sell into slavery a man of color who had remained in residence longer than one year after his manumission. As the overseers intended, this shot across the bow apparently produced an exodus of "several hundred" free Black people.

The overseers then threatened to sell all Black people who had violated the expulsion law of 1806; eight were actually sold, though one of them was allowed to sue (successfully) to recover his freedom. There was clearly a desire on the part of some, perhaps many, white residents in Accomack to push Black people out, but differences emerged about how far to pursue this project of ethnic cleansing: Accomack remained at or near the top of the list of Virginia counties in free Black population throughout the antebellum period.[21]

Other outbursts of repression occurred precisely when one would expect—most prominently after Nat Turner's slave revolt in 1831, in which at least fifty-five white people were killed. An unknown number of free Black people were physically attacked or driven away, especially in Southampton County, where the revolt had taken place. Despite the monetary stake slaveholders had in their human property, some enslaved Black people in and around Southampton—perhaps three dozen—were murdered in the aftermath of the rebellion. Reprisals against free Black people were limited; one man was executed, one was murdered, and one free Black rebel took his own life rather than be captured.[22]

Even a crisis of this magnitude could expose different shades of opinion underlying the white supremacist consensus. Some local militia officers beyond Southampton and adjacent counties thought they detected hints of free Black restiveness after the Turner revolt, while others believed the opposite and tried to maintain calm. The governor of Virginia and the less excitable local leaders in 1831 strove to get firearms to poorly equipped local militiamen but also to stop attacks against innocent free and enslaved Black people and "to quiet the publick mind." Five free Black men were charged with having participated in the Nat Turner revolt, but only one of those was convicted and executed. Only one free Black man had been among those prosecuted after Gabriel's attempted rebellion in 1800.[23]

Still, the Turner rebellion immediately produced a ratcheting up of other kinds of repression aimed at free and enslaved Black people. Local patrols now rode Virginia's rural byways more frequently. Large numbers of free Black people who had not regularly renewed their registrations did so now, whether out of newfound caution or under direct pressure from whites; some registered for the first time.

HORRID MASSACRE IN VIRGINIA.

The Scenes which the above Plate is designed to represent, are---Figure 1. a Mother intreating for the lives of her children. ---2. Mr. Travis, cruelly murdered by his own Slaves.---3. Mr. Barrow, who bravely defended himself until his wife escaped. ----4. A company of mounted Dragoons in pursuit of the Blacks.

Just Published, an Authentic and Interesting

NARRATIVE

OF THE

TRAGICAL SCENE

Which was witnessed in Southampton county (Virginia) on Monday the 22d of August last, when FIFTY FIVE of its inhabitants (mostly women and children) were inhumanly massacred by the Blacks!

Short and imperfect sketches of the horrid massacre above mentioned have appeared in the public Journals, but the public are now presented with every particular relative thereto, communicated by those who were eye witnesses of the bloody scene, and confirmed by the confessions of several of the Blacks while under sentence of death.

A more shocking instance of human butchery has seldom occurred in any country, and never before in this—the merciless wretches carried destruction to every white person they found in the houses, whether the hoary head, the lovely virgin, or the sleeping infant in the cradle! they spared none!—a widow (Mrs. Whitehead) and her 10 children were murdered in one house! among the slain on that fatal night, was an amiable young lady but 17 years of age, who the day following was to have been united in marriage to a young gentleman of North-Carolina, who had left home the evening preceding with the expectation of conveying there the succeeding day the object of his affections! but, alas! how sad was his disappointment! he was the third person who entered the house after the horrid massacre, to witness the mangled remains of her whom he was so shortly to espouse! The Blacks after having completed their work of death, attempted to evade the pursuit of those who had collected to oppose them, by secreting themselves in a neighboring swamp, to the borders of which they were pursued by a company of mounted dragoons. Of the fifty five slain nearly two thirds of the number were children, not exceeding twelve years of age! and it was truly a melancholly scene (as was observed to the writer by one who witnessed it) to behold on the day of their interment so great a number of coffins collected, surrounded by the weeping relatives!

While the friends of humanity however or wherever situated, cannot but sincerely and deeply lament the awful destruction of so many innocent lives, yet, the humane and philanthopic citizens of New-England, and of the middle States, cannot feel too thankful for the repose and peace of conscience which they enjoy, by wisely and humanely abolishing laws dooming a free born fellow being (without fault or crime) to perpetual bondage!---an example truly worthy of imitation by our brethren at the South.

The Narrative (which contains every important particular relating to the horrid massacre) is afforded for the **trifling sum of 12 1-2 Cents.**

☞ This paper left for perusal, and to be returned when called for.

"Horrid Massacre in Virginia . . . in Southampton County," 1831, broadside. *VMHC*

A bizarre illustration of these varying white responses to the Turner revolt came in Prince Edward County. The county court rather belatedly ordered the confiscation of weapons owned by free Black people. But the order was executed only in certain parts of the county; the authorities auctioned off those weapons that were collected but then paid out the proceeds (minus a constable's commission) to the Black former owners.[24]

The Turner revolt led to an intense discussion in the Virginia General Assembly of the future of slavery. Proposals for very gradual, compensated emancipation accompanied by removal of freed Black people ultimately failed. Instead, those white Americans who promoted colonization as a device to expatriate *already-free* Black people rather than as a means to promote new manumissions saw their hand strengthened. Restrictions on Black life that had been codified in 1801 or even earlier were now reinforced and added to.

Serious though this reactionary wave was, the level of white vigilance that followed Turner's rebellion waned in a matter of months. Patrolling, free Black registrations or renewals, and other indices of repression in many parts of the state returned to previous levels. Manumissions, though much less frequent than in the late 1700s and early 1800s, still sometimes occurred, even as the national agitation over slavery exacerbated tensions during the 1850s.[25]

Anne S. Rice of Hampden-Sydney, a devout Presbyterian who kept a biography of British abolitionist William Wilberforce on her bookshelf, freed and sent to Liberia three enslaved families and several other individuals. John Watson left an exceptional will in 1855 in which he manumitted his sixty-seven enslaved people and provided money to establish them in Liberia. When Watson's white heirs challenged the will, a jury upheld his bequest; Watson's executors spent some $9,000 transporting the freedpeople to Africa and providing new clothing and $60 in gold for each of them.[26]

From 1831 to 1860, manumissions became more frequent in Richmond—there were more than 350 of them in those years—even as the number dwindled in most rural counties. These urban manumissions typically formalized self-purchases by enslaved Black people who had laboriously earned the price of their freedom.[27]

Older histories assert that most free Black people worked at the same sorts of jobs enslaved people did, and that members of the two groups often worked and lived side by side. This is true but also somewhat misleading, in that the statements are intended to suggest that freedom made little difference in the working lives of Black people—that free and enslaved alike were confined to menial labor in squalid conditions.

"The plantation police or home-guard examining Negro passes on the levee road below New Orleans," F. B. Schell, from *Frank Leslie's Illustrated Newspaper*, July 11, 1863. *Library of Congress*

In fact, significant numbers of free and enslaved Black people worked at skilled occupations. Partly because of the availability of slave labor, there was often an oversupply of people plying certain skilled occupations in antebellum Virginia. Yet many free Black shoemakers, blacksmiths, carpenters, coopers, and midwives competed successfully, supporting themselves and their families. Various categories of work, especially in the construction trades, were often carried out by racially integrated crews. Crops were frequently harvested by white, free Black, and enslaved men working together, with the free laborers of both races often earning identical wages.[28]

Many free Black women worked at spinning, weaving, knitting, and sewing, but there are indications that they preferred to work in their own homes and sell some of what they produced rather than work under white supervision. Domestic service in white people's houses—a mainstay of Black women's employment in the decades after emancipation—was far less common among Virginia's free Black women before the Civil War. With the passage of time, more and more free Black people worked in small (and some not so small) factories in places such as Richmond, Petersburg, and Farmville, where they processed and packed chewing tobacco alongside enslaved workers.

Some free Black children, like more than a few white youngsters, found themselves apprenticed, almost always to white people. These apprenticeships were often ordered by local overseers of the poor when those authorities asserted that a family was not capable of rearing a child properly. Apprentices worked under their designated masters and received no compensation apart from food, shelter, and a one-time payment upon completing their term (at age twenty-one for men, eighteen for women). Some apprenticeships were mainly exploitative, but others equipped young free Black people, primarily men, to ply gainful trades for a lifetime.[29]

Many free Black Virginians performed agricultural work, typically alongside enslaved workers on land owned by white people. But some free Black people tilled land they themselves owned. Nineteenth-century rural Virginia was an environment in which many people—white and Black, rich, middling, and poor—pursued more than one occupation, and this was particularly true of free Black people who cultivated their own land. In the runup to his manumission, Hercules White, Sr., of Cumberland and Prince Edward worked at carpentry, coopering (making barrels), carting wood, slaughtering hogs, salting and storing meat, and growing corn and tobacco.[30]

Various members of Hercules White's extended family, several of his neighbors, and numerous other free and enslaved Black men in Piedmont Virginia worked as boatmen. In the white popular imagination, probably no occupation was more thoroughly associated with free Black men, even though white men pursued it, too. The crew of a batteau included a headman (tillerman) and two boatmen propelling a long, narrow vessel using poles pressed into the river bottom. The batteaux carried crops—mostly grain and tobacco—down the rivers of the Piedmont region to Virginia's fall line cities, especially Richmond and Petersburg. Then they returned upstream, hauling manufactured goods and supplies.

Boatmen were by definition highly mobile, and Black crews often worked without white supervision; that sort of latitude aroused anxiety among some white people. Lawmakers adopted legislation that purported to restrict, for example, where Black boatmen might land during their voyages, but these

"Black boatmen," Benjamin Henry Latrobe, watercolor. *Courtesy of Library of Virginia*

laws seem to have been enforced only rarely if at all. A significant number of free Black men managed to purchase their own batteaux. By 1850, Black men owned one-third of the forty-one boats running the Appomattox River out of Farmville, and they carried nearly 40 percent of the freight that went into and out of that town by water. Three of the top five boat owners were Black.[31]

Other free Black people likewise achieved impressive economic success. Black women attained prominence in Petersburg as property owners and entrepreneurs. Willis Madden, a free man of color, worked his way up from blacksmithing, shoemaking, and wagoning to become a man of prominence in Culpeper County in north-central Virginia; in the later antebellum years, he owned a thriving farm, a tavern, a general store, a forge, and a wagoning business. Samuel Johnson bought his own freedom, purchased his family, acquired significant property in and around Warrenton, and "lived his final years in something approaching refinement."[32]

In Campbell County on the edge of the Blue Ridge, Robert Wright, free man of color and prosperous, slaveholding farmer with a white wife, was held in high regard by his white neighbors. "For many if not most important purposes, class and economic condition, rather than race, constructed his identity," historian Thomas Buckley found. Other historians of free Black life along Virginia's Blue Ridge have likewise uncovered patterns similar to those in the lower Piedmont and Tidewater. Significant numbers of free Black people bought land, practiced skilled trades, moved about, and renewed their registrations only sporadically. They typically sought independence from white people while necessarily interacting with them frequently; some, perhaps many, were employed by whites.[33]

Local courts in and near the Blue Ridge generally treated free Black people as judiciously as was possible in a system that barred Black people from serving as jurors and from testifying against white defendants. In a study of free Black life in Lynchburg, historians Ted DeLaney and Phillip Wayne Rhodes found the familiar inconsistency between the general and the specific in the attitudes of white people, concluding that free Black folk "were generally hated as a class, although often beloved and praised as individuals."[34]

The economy was not the only factor promoting contact between white and Black Virginians. Social, moral, and religious values sometimes drew white and free Black people together, while alienating each group from less "respectable" members of their own race. Black and white members of rural Christian churches represented a large fraction of the population (though not a majority, contrary to what many assume today); they worshipped together, albeit in racially segregated spaces and under white pastors. White and Black Christians in rural churches suffered together when white men sometimes harassed the devout and disrupted services.[35]

Free Black people such as the White family of Israel Hill, the Maddens of Culpeper, Samuel Johnson of Warrenton, and Robert Wright of Campbell attained their economic successes by living out a work ethic that equaled or exceeded that of leading whites—who themselves often disprove our stereotypes of slaveholder indolence. Achievers, both white and free Black, sometimes expressed contempt for those of their own race whom they regarded as lazy or morally deficient.

The White family of Prince Edward brought Mely Howard, a fellow manumittee, into their home as a maid; Sam White later denounced her "bad behaviour" and the "utter worthlessness" of her husband, which, in the words of an eviction suit brought by White, differentiated the Howards "from the honest and industrious." Some of that wording may have come from Sam White's attorney, but the attitudes are clearly White's own. His family, devout Baptists, had earlier joined forces with a number of white fellow believers to establish the first Baptist congregation in Farmville; white and free Black members of that church frequently did business with one another.[36]

There were many other cultural affinities that linked Black and white Virginians. The everyday speech of white people, including many prominent individuals, resembled Black vernacular English in various ways. Many white and Black people measured time by the sun and by the seasonal cycles of nature and of agriculture rather than with timepieces and calendars. Names given to Black and white children were more similar than they have been in recent times. Numerous people of both races believed in the efficacy of folk medicine derived in part from African and African American traditions.[37]

Free and enslaved Black people sometimes socialized with white people. Other whites might grumble or even file official complaints when that happened, but white society in rural Virginia seems often to have tolerated those who played cards with Black folk or entertained them "frequently." In Albemarle County, free men of color, many of whom had fought for the United

States in the Revolutionary War, operated in "a relatively easy-going interracial social order" that encompassed economic, social, and sexual life.[38]

The realm of interracial sex included permanent spousal unions between men of color and white women. Such marriages were almost never legally recognized, and we know about these spousal partnerships largely through court records generated when some white person complained about them. But it appears that such relationships were rarely broken up or punished.[39]

The contours of day-to-day life among free Black Virginians have often been misunderstood because the tenets of white supremacy were more uniform than was the day-by-day application of that racist worldview. White people in Virginia, as in the United States generally, had no doubt that they should and would rule society. Many assumed that free Black people as an aggregate population constituted a problem and perhaps a danger. Yet, many of those same whites dealt routinely, sometimes even cordially, with free Black individuals whom they knew personally. Free Black people in other parts of the state could seem sinister even while those in one's own neighborhood were an accepted if disadvantaged part of the environment.

White and free Black people in Virginia thus interacted and even cooperated in many realms—with crucial exceptions, including the organs of governance and any other situation that would have placed a Black person in a position of authority over whites. Ironically, such friendly relations as did arise between white and free Black people probably shored up white supremacy by encouraging whites to see their social system as less abusive than it was in fact. White Americans' belief in their own friendliness toward, and even "love" for, individual Black people would have a similar self-justifying effect from emancipation to the present.

A particular kind of white-Black relationship came into view when, from time to time, free Black individuals petitioned the General Assembly to exempt them from any possibility that the expulsion law of 1806 would be used against them. These petitions show that some free Black people saw the law as an actual threat rather than a dead letter, but they also demonstrate that Black petitioners could win widespread and fervent support from large numbers of influential white people who wrote testimonials on their behalf.

The petitions illustrate how free Black Virginians influenced white public opinion. Political lobbying or protest were not live options for them. But neither did most of them actively seek protection from paternalistic whites, as some historians have said. The standing of these petitioners and of other free Black Virginians rested on what they achieved economically and morally and the way they carried themselves generally. The respect that many Black people won helps explain the frequent non-enforcement of anti-free Black laws.

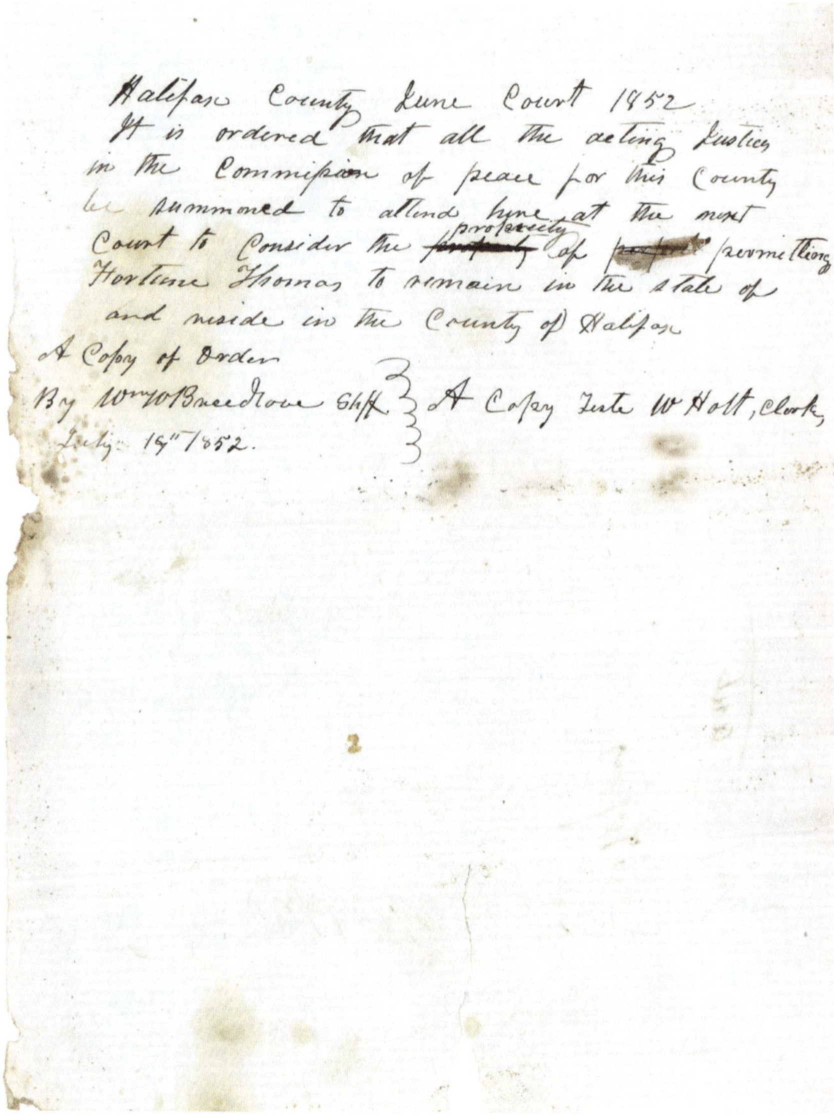
Halifax County June Court 1852
It is ordered that all the acting Justices in the Commission of peace for this County be summoned to attend here at the next Court to Consider the propriety of permitting Fortune Thomas to remain in the State of and reside in the County of Halifax
A Copy of Order
By Wm W Breedlove Shff } A Copy Teste W Holt, Clerk,
July 14th 1852.

Petition of Fortune Thomas, a free Black man, to remain in Virginia, July 14, 1851. *VMHC*

Some have concluded that white men supported these free Black petitioners for economic reasons; and the whites' testimonials do typically invoke the Black supplicants' material services to local economies. Indeed, the petitions have been cited as evidence that free Black people were economically indispensable to the communities in which they lived. But skilled workers were abundant in much of the state; for this and other reasons, Virginians were leaving the Commonwealth in large numbers during the antebellum years. Thus, even if every skilled free Black person had somehow joined the exodus, the effect on the economy would have been limited and temporary. The economic "usefulness" of free Black petitioners, real though it was, seems to have been cited in the petitions on the tactical assumption that arguments of economic utility would carry more weight with legislators than those based on morality or personal affinity would.

A seldom remembered feature of Virginia's legal system is that, despite the ban on Black testimony against whites, free Black people could file civil lawsuits just as white people did, even if the defendant was white. This right could become particularly important if a white person attacked a free Black individual and no white witnesses were available to sustain a criminal case against the offender. In Prince Edward County between 1800 and 1861, more than a dozen free Black men and women sued white persons who they said had assaulted them; those Black plaintiffs' record of winning their suits and receiving significant awards was lower, but not drastically so, than that for white people suing other whites. Free Black people sometimes sued whites for other reasons, too—in disputes involving property or unpaid debts, for example. Occasionally, one free Black Virginian sued another.

Legal actions filed by free Black people sometimes reveal vivid details about everyday life. On August 5, 1819, six Appomattox River batteaux had to delay their downriver voyage when they encountered an obstruction that a mill owner had caused at a place called Stony Point. Three weeks later, the same six boats—now making the return trip upstream—ran up against the same obstruction once again, all of them on the same date. The boat owners—one of whom was a free Black man—went to court to seek a monetary judgment against the proprietor of the mill. The chronology laid out in the lawsuit suggests that Black and white boatmen were traveling the river together on these two occasions, and they may have done the same on other voyages as well.[40]

One highly specialized type of lawsuit could, with a court's permission, be filed by enslaved people suing for their freedom—often based on claims that they were descended not from enslaved Black women but rather from improperly enslaved Virginia Indians. From time to time, such permission was granted and a claim to freedom sustained, augmenting very slightly the number of free Black people in the Commonwealth. In a single such case in Prince Edward, the superior court freed about forty people in 1814.[41]

The 1850s saw another rise in white anxiety about free Black people. Suspicion centered on individuals who had left the state, spent time in the North, and then returned. Such people, it was thought, might have absorbed abolitionist ideas, which they might now try to disseminate in Virginia. The threat or the reality of legal action induced at least some of these Black people to leave the state once again.

Some free Black Virginians now began to worry that the expulsion law of 1806 might come to be more generally enforced. In Richmond, more Black individuals applied for waivers of the expulsion requirement in the 1850s, and a higher percentage of those petitions were denied than in earlier years. Some of the few free Black people in certain localities who faced an imminent threat of expulsion responded by requesting permission to enslave themselves to white people; the General Assembly passed a law in 1856 that permitted them to do so.[42]

Self-enslavement has been cited as evidence that oppression of free Black people had become so unbearable that some preferred slavery itself. In fact, however, only about a hundred people invoked this law, and some of them, perhaps many, did so in concert with white prospective "masters" who had agreed with them in advance that the arrangement would exist solely on paper. A provision of the law that explicitly prohibited this kind of collusion was routinely ignored. Still, the fact that even a few now felt the need to protect themselves against possible expulsion attests to rising pressure on free Black people as tensions over slavery roiled the nation.[43]

In the 1850s, as after the Turner rebellion, additional repressive laws aimed at free Black people were adopted in Virginia. Yet the three decades following 1831 also saw noteworthy gains in free Black property-holding in the Commonwealth as in much of the South—another reminder that laws by themselves do not necessarily offer a reliable depiction of lived reality.[44]

The 1850s did bring renewed talk of ridding Virginia of its free Black population, but such proposals drew spirited and successful white opposition. Three Richmond newspapers opposed a bill introduced in the General Assembly in 1853 that would have hired out free Black people to involuntary labor, used the proceeds to remove them from the state, and sold into slavery any who remained after five years. Only a legislature "divested of all humanity" could pass such a law, said the *Dispatch*. Without questioning white supremacy as an overarching system, the editorialist averred that the free Black population included "many men of industry, intelligence, and general good character," adding that "the loafing free negro is not half so bad as the loafing white man, because he is much more afraid of the law, and much more amenable to reason."[45]

As North-South tension erupted into civil war, free Black people participated in the conflict in a variety of ways. The Confederacy introduced military conscription for white men only during the war's second year, but free Black men were drafted from the beginning of hostilities. They were assigned to laboring details—digging trenches, building fortifications, burying the dead—and were often stationed far from their homes. They were supposed to receive modest wages, but sometimes their pay was dispensed erratically.[46]

It would have been perilous for free Black people to appear disloyal to Virginia or to the Confederacy; some white people even believed that free Black men should and would participate in the southern war effort. "The free colored population . . . are ready and willing to do anything that they be called upon to do in the present emergency," said the *Richmond Dispatch* in 1861. A white resident of Petersburg informed the governor that "one hundred (100) free negroes[,] the pick of the place, good and true men[,] will offer their Services to the State & ask me to command them." One wonders whether this man's assessment was accurate or reflected wishful thinking born of his desire to become an officer. In any event, Black men were not accepted in the Confederate armies.[47]

Despite the risks, significant numbers of free Black men and women apparently aided the Union forces. The ranks of Black teamsters, cargo haulers, clothes washers, and the like who supported the federal army surely included some who had been free before the war. Other free Black men brought their knowledge of their Virginia homeland and its people to bear, serving as scouts, spies, or "agents."

A Warm Breakfast Winter
The Chief Cook.
An Evening Meal : Summer Camp.

"The Chief Cook," Edwin Forbes, 1861–65, pen and ink drawing. *VMHC*

A Union officer on the Peninsula reported in 1862 that "many free negroes can be found who could be fully trusted with the transmission of messages in cipher [code]." A Massachusetts cavalry officer considered his free Black guide "true as steel" and "found the colored people almost always to be so." He added that the information they provided "was invariably correct and often of the highest importance." A Confederate general defending Richmond corroborated these Yankee opinions, noting that free Black men were making themselves "dangerous" by serving as "good river pilots" for the invading federal forces.[48]

The end of the war brought general emancipation. As a practical matter, the process of liberation in Virginia had occurred in stages beginning in 1861 in areas controlled by Union forces, such as Fort Monroe on the lower Peninsula. After freedom for Black Virginians came definitively in 1865, conservative white lawmakers in the General Assembly adopted new measures that granted certain civil rights to the formerly enslaved, but which also limited the freedoms available to them.

The federal Reconstruction Acts of 1867 ushered in a new era of Black enfranchisement and participation in the political process. Many Black Virginians who had been free before the war brought into play the experience, skills, and financial resources they had acquired in prewar days, becoming successful entrepreneurs, teachers in Black schools, and political leaders. Those endeavors were replicated by many newly emancipated people.

Any present-day evaluation of free Black life in old Virginia is necessarily shaped both by the evidence that the past itself offers and by our own experience and values. Free Black Virginians were relegated to second- or third-class citizenship. Their white neighbors could not have imagined trading places with them (except, perhaps, for poor whites, themselves long disenfranchised in law and always marginalized in effect, who may have envied the most prosperous free people of color). When we compare the lives of free Black

Virginians with our own, the disabilities and insults their white neighbors imposed on them are painfully obvious.

Modern sensibilities prompt us both to detail the tyranny under which Virginia's free Black people lived and to recognize their many accomplishments. Indeed, it is tempting to frame the history of the Commonwealth's free Black people as a counterpoint between seamless oppression and dauntless resistance. But in fact unremitting oppression *does* daunt people; if it is severe enough, it can make resistance all but impossible.

To embrace the thesis of free Black achievement, then, requires us to accept certain distinctions between white racial ideology—crucial though it was—and the varieties of actual white behavior that we find in old Virginia. White Virginians showed again and again that they knew how to oppress; the social system they built proves it abundantly. From early on, one would have been hard-pressed to find a white person in Virginia who did not take it for granted that white domination generally and slavery specifically would and must continue. But within that consensus, daily life, full of tiny decisions and non-decisions, was acted out.

Most studies of free Black life in recent years have examined geographic areas small enough to allow deep dives into primary sources, especially local court records. A remarkable number of these works involve Virginia localities. They depict vividly the civil disabilities and racist propaganda that beset free Black people before 1865 without letting victimhood define those people. And they recognize the intricacies of Virginia's interracial history.

White people's vacillations and distractedness, along with ties of culture, interest, and even affection between white and free Black individuals, created certain openings within a system whose benighted racial credo seemed to rule out any sort of flexibility. The ambition and the ingenuity of free Black Virginians equipped them to find those openings and to make the most of them, writing a remarkable record of achievement within a surprisingly complex white supremacist society.

"Hampton, Virginia. Slab-town," December 1864, stereographic photograph. *Library of Congress*

H
C
eau Minéral
B
B
JAMES

Chapter 2

The Christian Faith and Legacies of Liberation in Virginia's Free Black Society

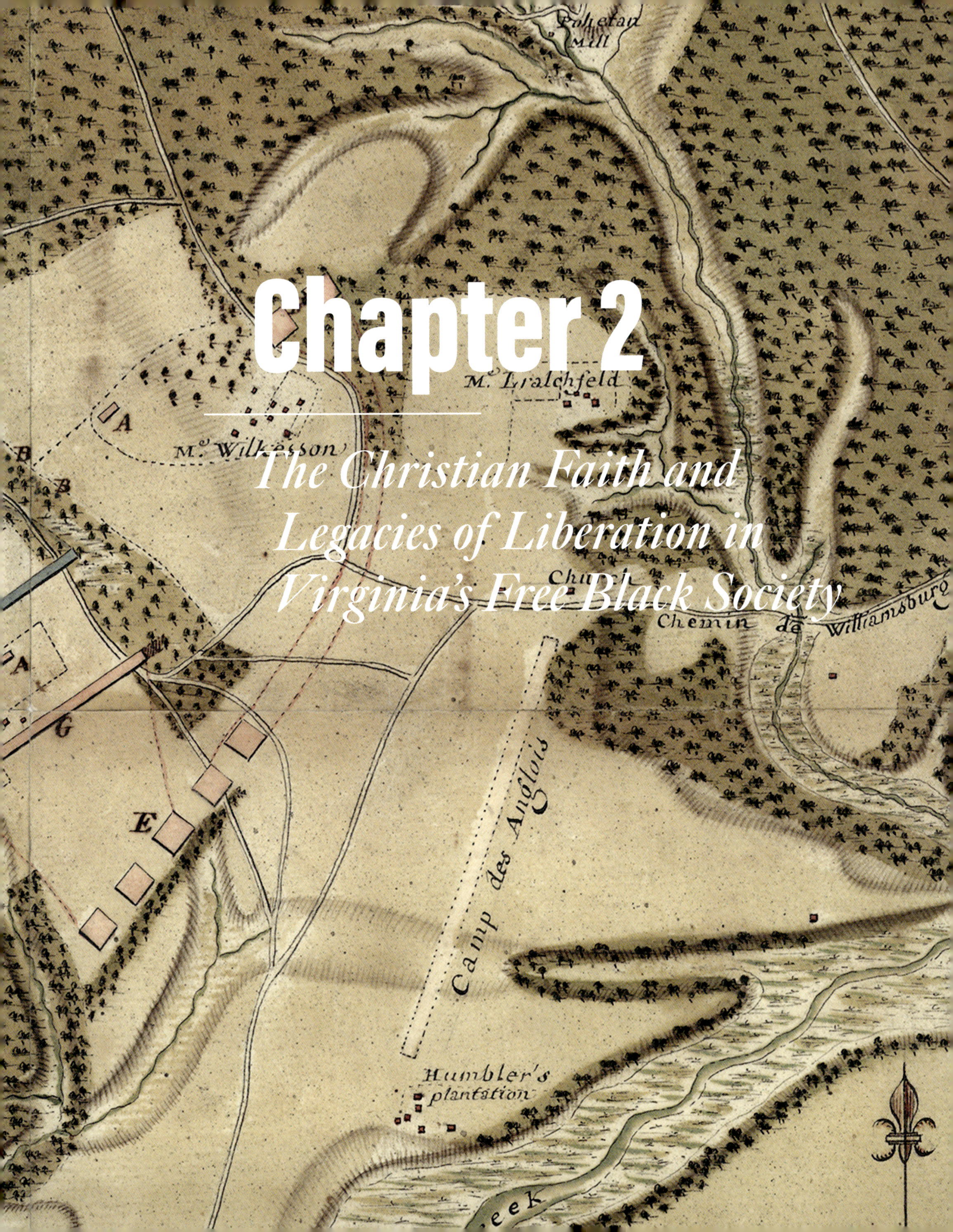

2

The Christian Faith and Legacies of Liberation in Virginia's Free Black Society

Evanda S. Watts-Martinez

The peculiar realities of free Black people during the eighteenth and early nineteenth centuries continue to intrigue those observing the evolution of North America. As historical researchers examine the ways in which these people's lived experiences operated in adjunct to those in bondage, the lesser-known accounts of the lives of freed people have prompted historians and thinkers in various fields to learn more about their presence, influence, and contributions in the societal, cultural, political, economic, and legal contexts of early America. Also important to some observing the free Black ethos in early Virginia is a faith tradition that had shaped their identities, empowered their resilience, and fueled their resistance against oppression since before the eighteenth century. As the cornerstone for free Black Virginians' lives since the seventeenth century, the Christian faith tradition provided both spiritual sustenance and a framework for their stance against systemic oppression. Thus, inspiring the contributions and legacies of Virginia's free Black people was a life-sustaining religious belief system that fortified them in the face of socio-political structures that denied their humanity, restricted their lives, and deprived them of their rights.

This discussion explores the Protestant Christian movement in Virginia and focuses on its historical role, evolution, and influence in the lives of free Black people. Also observed are the ways in which their Christianization prompted a theological reanalysis of a religious system that justified the inferiority and subjugation of their race. Central to understanding the dynamics of free Black society in the eighteenth and early nineteenth centuries is recognizing the persistent challenges arising because of their racial identities. Constant references to their race subjected free Black Virginians to ongoing racism and discrimination, continually reminding them of their societal limitations.

Before the intensification of racial distinction and the entrenchment of chattel slavery in Virginia, some early Africans arrived as indentured servants and were able to socialize, work with, and "enjoy many of the same rights as free whites." In his historical study of free Black people in Virginia, John H. Russell noted that by the mid-seventeenth century, those who were free continued to be referenced by their race while facing restrictions and being reduced in their societal status as people. With the society shifting toward race-based enslavement, free Black people adjusted themselves among populations of whites, Black slaves, and indigenous people, although they were constantly reminded that, though they were not enslaved, their "freedom" was not sufficient to make them the social equals to Virginia's white colonists.[1]

The pseudo freedom among free Black Virginians influenced their Christian experiences in early America as their conversion, baptism, and religious perspectives mostly served to help them endure the duress of the dehumanization of slavery, subjugation, and oppression. The anomaly of these lived experiences placed them in the position of existing in a society in which living free eluded them, as they operated precariously among both tolerant and intolerant white people. Accordingly, living outside of the institution of enslavement was not akin to freedom, in a society in which Black men and women were all too often presumed to be slaves. The experiences of living free amid racial intolerance and oppression extend back to the seventeenth century, and continued to evolve over time. As the distinction between indentured servants (who were often white) and enslaved Africans grew, the lives of free people of African descent, particularly mixed-race individuals, complicated the notions of race and social status in Virginia.

Further complicating the societal norms were free Black people who had converted to Christianity. As the century progressed, they were subjected to racial prejudice and discrimination as societal attitudes, laws, and practices changed. Elizabeth Key Grinstead's story is a powerful example of the precarious nature of freedom for Black Christians, specifically mixed-race individuals, during that time. Grinstead was born in 1630 in Warwick County, Virginia to an enslaved African woman (Martha) and a British man (Thomas Key) from England. She grew up as an indentured servant. Thomas Key, who came to the Virginia colony in 1616, became a tobacco planter and eventually served in the Virginia House of Burgesses. Elizabeth's godfather, a prominent politician, took her into his home after her father's death. She was treated like an indentured servant and then sold to a judge in Northumberland County, who considered her as his slave. After the judge's death, she sued his estate for her freedom, and this suit was backed by her claim of inheriting the status of her English father under the British law which at that time governed the early American colonies. She finally presented a certificate of baptism as evidence of her Christianity, which meant at the time "under British law that she could not be enslaved." Grinstead, one of the first Black women in the colonies to sue for her freedom and win, lived a life prior to and after the establishment of slavery, yet she was not truly free. The intricate nature of her social status led to the ensuing actions of Virginia legislators who passed several new laws stating that, whether enslaved or free, a child of a white man and an African woman was to be defined by the mother's status.[2]

An additional law was passed to reinforce the idea that the declaration of conversion to Christianity did not make an enslaved Black person free. These pieces of legislation reified the indelible mark of servitude and enslavement that loomed over the lives of free Black Virginians, including those who had received instruction in Christian religion since before the middle of the seventeenth century. The value of Christian conversions among free Black people, such as Elizabeth Key Grinstead, arouses curiosity about the impact of Christianity and the baptism of free Black people in a slaveholding colonial society. Reflecting on a free community that once included a core group of Black people who worked, socialized, earned money, raised crops, kept livestock, and had access to the justice system in Virginia before the 1782 Manumission Act is significant. Such a reflection sets the stage for understanding the profound impact of faith on the lives of free Black Virginians.[3]

The observation of the faith journey that contributed to the rise of Christian consciousness among free Black people in Virginia includes the rejection of distorted religious views that mobilized racialized chattel slavery. It also includes a doctrinal transformation that affirms the humanity and the quest for freedom among people of African descent. Forwarded in this essay are themes of liberty and justice as conveyed via a reframed Christianity seen through the theological and Christological lenses of Virginia's free Black people, who used their new understanding of a faith tradition to make sense of their lives and give them hope. Centralizing the experiences of eighteenth- and early nineteenth-century free Black people in Virginia brings a focus to the historical discourse on the faith and actions of a lesser-known group of Christians in the Commonwealth who ignited and sustained their resistance to the prevalent oppressive systems. This approach provides meaningful information on a Christian perspective that challenged the limitations of their freedom, contributed to the flourishing of their spirituality, and blazed a trail for future Black movements and lasting liberation legacies.[4]

Christianization through Virginia's Revivals

Despite some Virginia planters' contempt for Black people and their stated opposition to religious instruction within communities of color, missionaries who journeyed through the state preached the Gospel to those who received the religion by the year 1747. The notion that Black people were equal to whites in God's eyes, and the intentions of preaching the Gospel to bring obedience to the enslaved, were conflicting ideas that were often conveyed by pastors. Although the era of the First Great Awakening (the 1730s and 1740s) demonstrated inconsistent actions regarding the inclusion of Black people, it initiated much contemplation about human liberties and religious freedom in the 1750s. During the late 1750s, the preaching tours assigned to itinerant missionaries resulted in the organization of new evangelical sites. Virginia became an organizing location for the Presbyterians, Methodists, and Baptists.

Free Black people were among those who attended the revivals and worshipped alongside white Virginians in their particular Christian denominations. By 1755, Presbyterian pastor Samuel Davies had baptized about one hundred Black people and had begun preaching the Gospel to those who had initially resisted the religion because of its association and alignment with their oppressors' belief systems. Nonetheless, Davies spoke to a circuit of congregants in Hanover, Goochland, Henrico, Caroline, and Louisa counties. He continued his religious instruction for Black Virginians who were eager to accept Christian knowledge and be baptized after a proper time designated for Christian instruction. It was estimated that at least 1,000 Black people attended the churches established by Davies, although the idea of bondage was not criticized by the enslaver himself.[5]

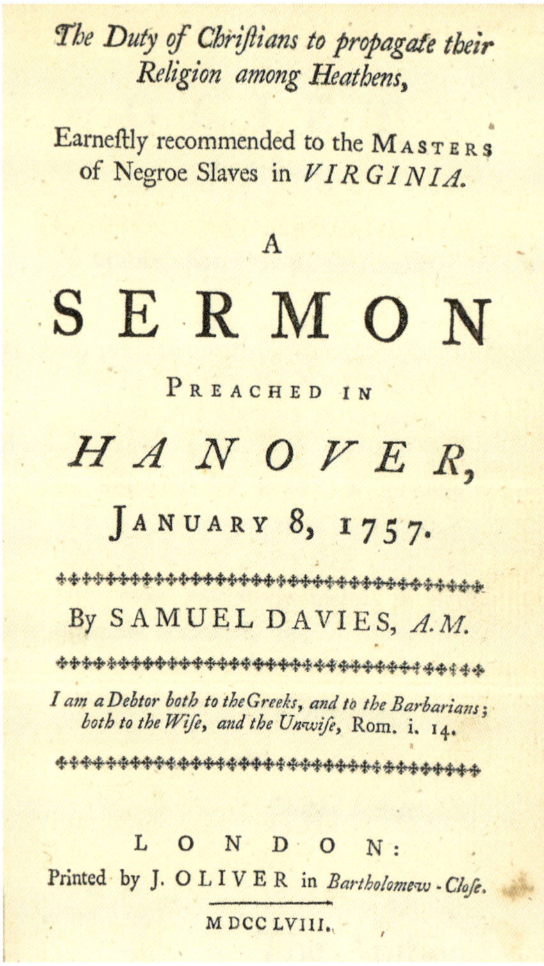
The Duty of Christians to propagate their Religion among Heathens,

Earnestly recommended to the MASTERS of Negroe Slaves in *VIRGINIA.*

A

SERMON

PREACHED IN

HANOVER,

JANUARY 8, 1757.

By SAMUEL DAVIES, *A.M.*

I am a Debtor both to the Greeks, and to the Barbarians; both to the Wise, and the Unwise, Rom. i. 14.

LONDON:
Printed by J. OLIVER in *Bartholomew-Close.*

MDCCLVIII.

The Duty of Christians to propagate their Religion among Heathens . . . A Sermon Preached in Hanover, Samuel Davies, January 8, 1757, printed pamphlet. *VMHC*

During the pre-Revolutionary period, Black people found initial acceptance within emerging white Christian churches, although the spirit of inclusion was neither consistent nor sustaining. Yet, the rise of Christian consciousness among the free Black population continued in the formulation of other denominations, which led to the great revival of Christianity in Virginia under the preaching of the Methodists who worked in connection with the pastors of the Episcopal church, which Black people attended in crowds. With the Christianization of Black people (both free and enslaved) spreading to fourteen counties, including Roanoke, the religious revivals were enjoyed and continued until 1791. Thousands were converted and baptized in the Methodist and Presbyterian traditions, although the number of Black conversions began to decline as the Presbyterian ministry transitioned from the public "revivalist camp meeting style" to an educational study setting and a conservative approach to Christian teaching. Conversely, an increased number of free Black Virginians joined the Methodist and Baptist churches during the revival seasons. As the Baptist congregation grew, a great majority of Black people within the denomination desired to hear ministers of their own race preach.[6]

Unbonded Black Virginians often identified their own worship locations, which offered a space of fellowship with enslaved people without the slaveholder's presence. Indeed, these secret worship services, particularly those held in Virginia, were opportunities for a reprieve from the inflictions of the harsh realities that were faced daily. The eighteenth-century Black church was the sacred place and often a secret escape into a world in which Christian consciousness-raising and a tradition of faith-strengthening presented life-affirming moments for spiritual expressions and connections that led Black congregants through meaningful bonding experiences. Worship environments, such as those located in the Virginia swamps, were available for the oppressed community to express their common and distinctive hardships.

Clandestine assemblies occurred among the Black population in the plantation South who gathered in worship meetings that were forbidden by law. Determined to heighten their Christian consciousness in environments led by Black preachers, they created signals, passwords, and messages undiscernible to white people. Unknown to enslavers in Virginia, the invisible churches were the unseen meeting locations that became "hush harbors," or the secluded locations in which Black people could include rhythmic African music, singing, and clapping as

"A Negro Camp Meeting in the South," Sol Eytinge, Jr., from *Harper's Weekly*, August 10, 1872, wood engraving. *Library of Congress*

a part of their evangelical expressions in their intense religious services. Ministers during this era who observed the experiences of Black Christians noted their "danced religion," or the religious emotions expressed through bodily movements.[7]

As early as 1770, free and enslaved Black communities sought to increase their Christian consciousness and express their own understanding of Christianity through their independent church communities, despite some resistance from enslavers who feared their conversion would lead to the freedom of enslaved Black people and the consequential threat to white society's economic status and social order. After the American Revolution, the Black Christian communities began to form, organize, and establish denominational churches, such as the African Methodist Episcopal Church and the African Methodist Episcopal Zion Church. After the American Civil War, the National Baptist Convention was established in the South. With slavery becoming more entrenched in the southern states, covert worship services continued in Virginia, where hush harbors or brush arbors remained operational for Black private worship services.

Peter Randolph (1825?–1897), frontispiece image in *From Slave Cabin to Pulpit: The Autobiography of Rev. Peter Randolph*, by Peter Randolph (Boston: J. H. Earle, 1893). *VMHC*

When observing the narratives of free Black people like Peter Randolph, who was freed from the institution of slavery in Prince George County in 1847, one can see how the hush harbor worship experience remained necessary for Black Virginians. Randolph's story highlights information regarding their covert religious services and prayer meetings held in the swamps, among themselves, at a time and location that were understood and shared by both the free and enslaved Black communities. Randolph noted that, after a space had been arranged for worship, a health and wellbeing check took place among congregants. Also, praying and singing occurred after the kind of preaching that built up excitement among worshippers who succumbed to God's spirit (the Holy Ghost) and fell to the ground in excitement. During the service, the community could momentarily rise above their suffering, except during the times when they discussed their weekly struggles. As they bade farewell, they promised each other that should they meet no more while on earth, they would strive to meet in heaven—a place where they would share eternal joy and freedom.[8]

Randolph mentioned that, to evade patrols, the individual who was first to arrive at the worship location would break the limbs from trees and place them in the direction of the worship space. In these established sacred locations, Christian consciousness became elevated through the experiences of singing and praying among groups of people who risked their lives to worship God under a veil of secrecy for the purpose of transcending their suffering. With a profound yearning for God's word, biblical understanding, and social cohesion, the Black church experiences led to a reformulated version of Christianity to include elements of West African religious expressions and traditions that energized the congregants' thinking around freedom and liberation.

The reshaped religious tradition stimulated a renewed sense of humanity among eighteenth- and early nineteenth-century Black people, in a society in which the oppressed believed that a liberating God was present, notwithstanding societal misalignment with the Divine's vision of human flourishing. Contemporary society was observed as a world that functioned in opposition to God's biblical account of liberating actions. White sympathizers sought to support the plight of free and enslaved Black people. For instance, the Quakers' advocacy for the religious training of the oppressed community sought to help prepare them for their freedom. Before the antebellum period, however, some Methodists and Baptists receded from their positions on abolition, based on their alliance with those who believed that slavery was a matter of civil regulation rather than a moral question. These movements led them to minister to the free and enslaved who were opposed to preaching against bondage. On the other hand, white ministers who continued to speak out against slavery attracted more Black people to their local meetings. They spoke against enslavement only to discover the extent to which a divide existed among those preachers who owned slaves, those who manumitted Black people, and those who did not own slaves but showed a high tolerance for the institution of bondage. These realities further complicated the relationships between Black and white Christians in Virginia by centralizing the ideological inconsistencies that existed among white Christians who believed in God but adhered to religious doctrines interpreted to support the notion of God's divine providence and commission for Black people to serve lives in slavery.[9]

The Emergence of the Free Black Christian Consciousness in Virginia

Free and enslaved Black people who established worship locations in Virginia were often acknowledged for their enduring faith, courage, and resilient spirits by historians who discovered the depth of their religious experiences and their longing for an organized church during the eras in which such gatherings were illegal. Amid the restrictions imposed on Black religious services by Virginia society, two young Black members of the New Lights assumed leadership roles and established the First African Baptist Church (or Bluestone Church) on William Byrd III's plantation in Lunenburg County in 1758. The Black New Lights ministers embraced the dynamic, passionate, and emotional preaching styles of early 1800s white traveling evangelists, such as Jonathan Edwards and George Whitefield, who rejected the more traditional and ostensibly uninspiring ideas of the Old Lights. They adopted new Christian philosophies and approaches to spreading God's words and messages around conversion, sin, atonement, and personal salvation through revival meetings held in the colonies. The Old Lights' preference for a rational, scientific, logical, and formal preaching style in an orderly worship service contributed to their skepticism of the informal, spontaneous, and emotive religious revivals that included the egalitarian views of Christianity upheld by the New Lights. In any case, the Black New

Jonathan Edwards (1703–1758),
after Joseph Badger (1708–1765),
n.d., oil on canvas.
Princeton University, gift of Dr. J. Pennington Warter, Class of 1942

Lights' message about the equality of all men who were created in the image of God mirrored the evangelical ideologies preached by Baptist revivalists. This message appealed to large numbers of free and enslaved Black people after the Great Awakening in the 1730s and 1740s, and continued through the eighteenth century in such locations as Prince George County.[10]

By 1756, faithful free Black church leaders in Prince George County had significantly contributed to the development and evolution of the Black Christian consciousness. Through their fellowship within the Baptist tradition, they cultivated a strong sense of community, culminating in the establishment of what became known as the First Baptist Church of Petersburg. The Petersburg area had the largest (3,224) free Black population in the South and a new church led by a Black minister (and later a white pastor assigned by the slaveholding community, which feared a slave revolt). Furthermore, Black Christians established worship spaces in Williamsburg. Before the Historic First Baptist Church of Williamsburg's founding in 1776, free Black itinerant preacher Reverend Moses, who was often captured and whipped for holding worship meetings, risked his life to construct a fellowship site at the Green Spring Plantation for the free and enslaved populations. Situated a few miles from town, the brush arbor location was a space for the Black community to pray, sing, and worship secretly in their own way. Its inclusive vision of honoring and glorifying God by obeying Jesus's command to make disciples of all people reflects an authentic connection to an ancestral heritage that encapsulated the idea of human dignity within an unambiguous free society. The church's enduring core values of unity, inclusiveness, and diversity inspire an observation of the evolution of the free Black Virginians' awareness of a faith tradition that formed a dichotomous relationship with the oppressors' God, who they believed to be aligned with the oppressed.[11]

Black Christian consciousness, or the understanding of the nature of God in the context of Black life, emerged from the lived experiences of people who refused to exalt a God of Black degradation. During the eighteenth century, Christianized Black freedmen in the Commonwealth questioned the nature of their religion, which presented an interpretation of a patriotic notion of a God who served oppression and brought death to Black people. Virginia's Black ministers, weary of the biblical notion of redemptive suffering, reinterpreted the scriptural accounts of God's nature to respond to oppression while

Green Spring Plantation appears in the upper left of Plan du Terrein à la Rive Gauche de la Rivière de James vis-à-vis Jamestown . . . , Jean Nicolas Desandroüins, 1781, map. *Library of Congress*

offering hope for deliverance by a divine Creator who expressed concern for believers living under such humiliating conditions as slavery and persecution. This message reflects the teachings of the Black New Lights ministers who journeyed to Petersburg—a city where growing levels of God-consciousness aligned with freedom and Christ's revolutionary teachings aimed at liberating downtrodden, marginalized, and oppressed communities.[12]

"A Christianized African," from *The History of the Negro Church*, by Carter G. Woodson (Washington, D.C.: The Associated Publishers, 1921), engraving. *VMHC*

Challenging the Limitations of Black Freedom: Faith and God-Consciousness

Enslaved Africans who landed in the Virginia colony set out to make their way to freedom and to fulfill their vision of living freely in order to enjoy the privileges of persons born free. Those who landed in Spain before coming to the colonies learned how to use the legal system for their liberation and hoped to use the colonial system to become free. As early as the seventeenth century, enterprising Black people had challenged the limitations of the colonial structure through the purchase of their freedom with a tobacco crop, livestock, or the labor of their children, as in the case of Thomas Webb who promised his enslaver John West of Accomack County in 1671 one thousand five hundred pounds of tobacco per year, a cow, a calf, and the service of his daughter to West's daughter until she became an adult. These and other agreements moved West to decide that Webb would be free after three years of service.[13]

By the early eighteenth century, Black men and women who converted to Christianity also sought freedom and were hopeful that their faith tradition would make their liberation possible. After discovering the legal measures that further subjugated their social status through restrictions imposed on the practice of manumission, Black people—particularly the converted—found themselves in a space in which a three-fold challenge to their freedom existed because of the color-based nature of slavery. First, Black freedom continued to be challenged through slave codes or a series of laws that reified the notion of Black people as property and cheap labor that had sustained the economy since the seventeenth century. Second, laws were enacted to control the behaviors and actions of an increasing population of enslaved people and allowed for their inhumane treatment on behalf of the slaveholding community. Whether manumitted by an act of legislature, by will and testament, or by deed, the third challenge to freedom was directed at the limited and tenuous liberties of free Black Virginians who lived in the shadows of slavery and under the assumption that people of African descent were only fit for servitude. As Virginia's slavery laws advanced, the social and industrial privileges of free Black people were curtailed as seen through the denial of voting rights, the inability to hold public office, travel restrictions, occupational boundaries, refusal of the right to bear arms, and denial of the right to bear witness of proof.[14]

After the arrival of the first laws dealing with the status of Black people in Virginia, those who were free found themselves living in a paradoxical social dynamic in which they were at liberty to move at will beyond their living quarters (though with travel limitations) but, unlike the enslaved, they relied on their own resources for survival. As perceived threats to the plantation economy and mainstream structure, Black people living with free social status were excluded from social equality. Indeed, their restricted social liberties and legal "privileges" did not imply constitutional rights. The restraints on freedom presented a difficult challenge for the entwined community of free and enslaved Black people, in a civilization that sustained ideals supporting the rigid association between blackness and enslavement. Despite the codes that formalized their subjugation, free Black people, who rarely considered their social status as higher than the enslaved, remained steadfast in their faith and determined to seek freedom for themselves and the bonded population. In the quest for their freedom and liberties, they brought in a religious tradition with a theological conception of a God who relates to, aligns with, and delivers the oppressed from the distress and afflictions that came with being Black, degraded, and disenfranchised in the slaveholding environment.[15]

Free Black ministers in the eighteenth century sought to shift society's consciousness away from equating blackness with enslavement. Instead, they advocated that Black minds, hearts, bodies, and souls belonged to God and were maintained and protected by way of God's divine providence. Through their tireless efforts, the aforementioned New Lights free Black ministers in Virginia were among the first organized evangelical messengers to challenge barriers to freedom through a biblically based notion of human equality, as they spread the gospel of liberation throughout the free and bonded Black communities in the central and southern regions of the state. These actions were necessary because most eighteenth-century evangelists failed to develop a clear theological view of race and ways to address the racialized thinking in the social, political, and legal institutions.[16]

This void in religious thought and spiritual consciousness left it to the ministers who represented oppressed communities to investigate the nature of God and formulate a God-conscious approach that acknowledged the existence of God's spirit and divine presence in all people. Furthermore, the God-conscious view of the Christian tradition offered an extensive understanding of salvation, redemption, and deliverance, while positioning theology against the degradations of the colonizers' and enslavers' racial politics and legalities.

For Black ministers in the Commonwealth, the God-conscious perspective in Christianity was needed to create space to produce the theological language that addressed Black humanity, the cruelties imposed upon them, and the hardships that influenced the development of their identity as Christians.

The reformulated religious tradition seems to have become a way for Virginia's New Lights Black ministers to present the divine Creator as a God of freedom and equality, and their congregants as people created for freedom and not slavery. Resulting from these theological notions were the regeneration and reclamation of the proud identities of Black people who became more determined to elevate their social status and challenge the existing social order. At the same time, as members of the free Black community continued to live under the Commonwealth's discriminatory laws, evangelizing from a doctrine of spiritual equality became prevalent in congregations that longed for complete freedom and sought comfort in the spiritual upliftment necessary for a momentary transcendence from degrading experiences.

Such ministers as Gowan Pamphlet, a tavern worker enslaved to Jane Vobe, owner of the King's Arms Tavern in Williamsburg, preached in clandestine gatherings in the arbors of the Green Spring Plantation. Following his predecessor, itinerant preacher Moses, Pamphlet shared messages of equality before God with a congregation of free Black and enslaved people in the 1770s. The New Lights' leanings in his messages provided the framework needed to challenge the prevailing notion that Black people's bondage was divinely ordained. Truly, the reverend's messages of freedom (he was granted his own in 1793) were a shift from the sermons of some of the evangelists of the earlier Christian revival traditions.

The Black New Lights' emphasis on compassionate worship did not separate God from sinful humans or position the Creator as an impersonal universal force who was an indifferent onlooker when it came to the struggles of racism. Because some evangelists in this era continued to deliver "fire and brimstone" salvation messages, their sermons did not speak against human bondage in the context of enslavement. This theological indifference continued to create space for justifying human oppression and its connection with economic wealth. The New Lights ministers challenged this position by offering a view of a God who desires to be in relationship with all people and a Creator who has sanctioned oppressed communities to live in their immutable right of freedom. Hence, the New Lights' call for human liberty concerned God's alignment with Black freedom and the Divine's intense love for vulnerable people in their lived experiences of struggle. As free Black men, the ministers were mindful that the people who functioned as barriers to freedom were those who consumed others without regard because of their economic agendas. This latter level of consciousness was regarded as operating outside of God's plan, placing privileged individuals in a precarious position with regard to a sovereign and omnipotent Creator whom the New Lights credited with possessing transformative universal power, which could include lifting the yoke of bondage off the shoulders of the enslaved to remove restrictive social, political, and legal burdens from the necks of oppressed communities without the consent of the prevailing establishment.[17]

The Imago Dei: A Theology That Challenges the Limitations of Black Freedom

The concept of the Imago Dei references humankind being made in God's image. This theological notion played a significant role in the communities of eighteenth-century Black ministers who were inspired by the New Lights evangelists' message of human equality. They seemed to have understood that the idea of being created in the image of God involves a sacred experience in which each person is declared as a child of the Lord and, therefore, freedom is bestowed upon everyone. This God-conscious view remained in the minds of a growing number of Black clergy, with the mission of debunking the paternalistic ideology that Black people's earthly suffering was a biblically based redemptive experience. As this scriptural misrepresentation of God's plan for Black people continued to fortify the oppressive societal systems, Black rights remained negated, especially among the free population who were unable to live out their freedoms fully and enjoy their human liberties in Virginia. Most converted Black people developed a spiritual perspective that emerged from their ancestry, cultural past, and lived experiences, which included Western evangelical teachings that guided their faith.[18]

With this perception of God's justice inspiring their biblical reflections, free Black Virginians led efforts to utilize a lens of equality as exemplified in God's creative order to challenge barriers to freedom in the Commonwealth. Biblical passages, such as Romans 6:15–23, provided a fuller view of slavery that enabled them to understand that African enslavement failed to reflect

God's calling for people's obedience and allegiance to Him alone. Further, the notion of servitude was neither spiritually substantiated nor aligned with the divine principles of love, justice, and mercy that led to the promise of eternal life. In effect, the discovery that all people were to be slaves of God and servants of the Lord's divine righteousness empowered a reevaluation of their circumstances through a spiritual lens that not only revealed the inconsistencies of the oppressors' interpretation of the scriptures, but also provided no biblical justification for their reigning dominion or the proclamation of being the agents of God for Black people. The image of God as depicted in Genesis 1:26–27 is captured in a single statement outlining God's charge to create humans in "our image and likeness." As a part of this plan, God's infinite and enduring love was perceived to be expressed in a creative process that placed the value and worth on people without regard for their ethnicity or background. Inspired by these biblical teachings, Minister Gowan Pamphlet admitted to waking up every day determined to prove that white people's ideas about Black people were erroneous. He stated that all people are endowed by God with unalienable rights, and that everyone should have them since it is impossible for one to pursue life, liberty, and happiness in chains. Such notions were upheld by free Black church leaders in Virginia, who faced the challenge of reconciling Jesus Christ as a Savior for Black people with a theology and understanding of Christ that were grounded in colonialism.[19]

Christocentric Consciousness: Challenging the Limitations of Black Freedom

The concept of Christocentric Consciousness reflects a view of Jesus Christ that was shared within and beyond the praise houses of the free and enslaved Christian communities. They believed that the benefits of adopting the same mindset as Christ would assist with their survival. Embedded in God's love and hope, Black people's Christ-centered and prophetic perspective led them to the level of spiritual maturity needed to envision and plan for their freedom and liberty amid the constraints on their lives. Setting their sights on Christ enabled them to look to Jesus for wisdom, enlightenment, guidance, and solutions to problems associated with being Black in the eighteenth and early nineteenth centuries' racist societies, with the expectation of an end to their sufferance.

With God's love linked to the fulfillment of the divine promise of deliverance, Black people considered Jesus's life and crucifixion to be intimately connected to their own insufferable living conditions. The alignment of Jesus's journey with the troubles of his followers gave the oppressed communities hope that their suffering was not in vain and would someday be crowned with the victory of freedom. As a paradigm of hope and freedom for Black Christians, Jesus's life stimulated considerable thought on his nature, message, and roles, and laid the groundwork for a life-affirming Christology that empowered an understanding of how his experiences coincided with Black subjugation. The Christ-centered lens became a tool to be used to verify communal identity through the blending of ancestral traditions with a retreaded Western faith religion. The meaningful union of the African and American faith traditions was factored into a relationship with God as enfleshed in Jesus, whose life and crucifixion stood against the dehumanizing actions of the forces that denied and limited the lives of the oppressed also during his own time.[20]

Jesus's Life and Message that Energized Black Freedom

Jesus, the embodied God of the poor, stood in solidarity with the socially outcast of society, and offered them hope and a sense of purpose while living out the fullness of his life. Existing in the Christocentric mindset of Black people (free and bonded) was the reciprocal and personal relationship between him and the oppressed who came to understand his humanity as Jesus and divinity as Christ. As a regenerative force in Black people's lives, Jesus was considered the son of the living and most high God and the Messiah who saved their souls and opened opportunities for all people to experience God's word. Known for his messages of love and compassion, Jesus emphasized kind treatment and empathy for others, regardless of their situations, circumstances, and backgrounds. Noted by the Black community was his handling of the humiliations, intimidations, threats, and mocking imposed by people in his society. Jesus's steadfastness throughout his ministry inspired strength. Moreover, his memorable message as framed in the Beatitudes from his Sermon on the Mount gave Black people the power to live in faith during difficult times and the ability to centralize God's higher law of love at work in their lives. The Beatitudes, including "Blessed are the poor in spirit, for theirs is the kingdom of heaven, Blessed are those who mourn, for they shall be comforted, Blessed are the meek for they shall inherit the earth," and "Blessed are you when people insult you, persecute you," provided a roadmap to a committed spiritual life

"Christ's Sermon on the Mount: The Parable of the Lily," Currier & Ives, 1866, lithograph. *Library of Congress*

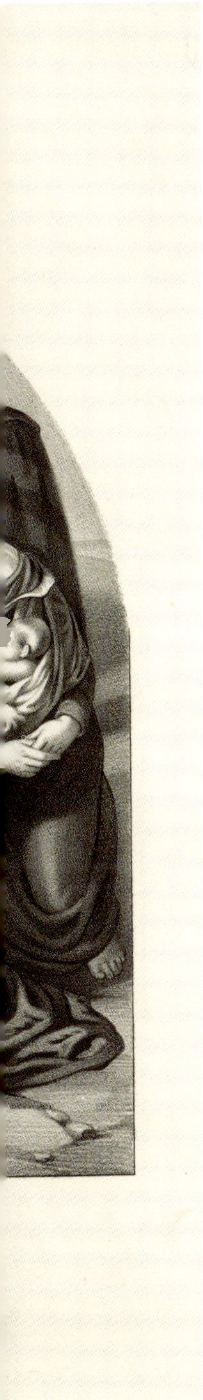

through their circumstances, and was a reminder that those holding God's kingdom in their hearts and minds could expect a new future to be in the present through Jesus Christ.

Jesus's message of hope was foundational in Virginia's Black faith community and served to motivate their movements toward freedom, however difficult the journey may have been. If the Savior's experiences of joy, frustration, pain, and concern for people were attributed to his humanity, then his connection with God—who gave him the spiritual and earthly authority to heal, sustain, and advance life—was evidence of his divinity. Accordingly, embedded in the Christocentric world view of Black people was the belief that the abolition of slavery would only occur through the influence of Jesus, the triumphant king, Lord, and Savior. Their Christ-centered theology placed Jesus as the authority over their lives. He was known as the Messiah, God's anointed son who had come as king and the supreme force to dethrone powerful existing structures and to denounce distressful actions that limited and devalued Black lives.[21]

Confessed in the covert congregations of Black Virginians in the eighteenth and early nineteenth centuries was Christ as their master who understood every stroke of the lash from the whip. Aptly known as "Sweet Jesus," which was the confirmation of the Savior's absolute ownership of their lives, he brought Black Christians a dose of sweetness in their bitter bondage of enslavement. The free Black people's Christocentric viewpoint brought to the foreground the cross that they continued to carry. For both the free and the bonded, an impractical compromise with subjugation added to their burdens. They held that the maltreatment on behalf of the slaveholding community was against God's convictions as well as in conflict with the mind of Jesus, and a renunciation of their rights and protections. Therefore, challenging the limitations of Black freedom denoted calling on the word of God to operate as the sword and shield that protected them from human torture—the "greatest of all tyrannies."[22]

Moved by Jesus's demonstration of love was the aforesaid Peter Randolph, who was the former slave of C. H. Edloe of Prince George County—a slaveholder who was apprehensive about holding people in bondage who believed in Christ. Estimated to have been born in 1825, Randolph recounted the moments of his manumission after his owner's death. He also highlighted his discovery of the story of Jesus's crucifixion, which led to his conversion. Randolph shared with the enslaved and his manumitted companions the narrative of the

FROM
SLAVE CABIN
TO PULPIT

Cover of *From Slave Cabin to Pulpit: The Autobiography of Rev. Peter Randolph*, by Peter Randolph (Boston: J. H. Earle, 1893). *VMHC*

passion and crucifixion of Jesus, and expressed his profound appreciation to his Savior for having all people in mind as he fulfilled the purpose for which he was born. Randolph's preachings expressed his gratitude for Christ having him in mind while suffering on the cross. He made a prophetic connection between the redemptive bloodshed of Jesus and the payment of a price that he—the former slave—could not pay. Hence, Jesus's death was viewed by the manumitted slave as Christ fulfilling the promise of his freedom.

In his moments of gratitude, Randolph placed Jesus in the center of his life and experienced a spiritual renewal and transformation that led to a Christocentric understanding of God's love as displayed through the passion of Christ. For him, the passion of Jesus reflected God's willingness to be adapted to each person's capacity through God's identification with humankind, via a servant who became obedient unto death. Randolph's Christian conversion experience, as inspired by the crucifixion, aligns with the notion that the cross speaks to oppressed people in ways that Jesus's life and teachings do not. In fact, some experts have discovered that during the course of the historical Christian movement, white missionaries preached the cross of Jesus to promote obedience, submission, and the suffering of Black people. Nevertheless, the free Black and enslaved communities in Virginia leaned on the cross to redeem their suffering and considered Christ's resurrection to be a prophetic notion of their future freedom.[23]

Revolutionizing Freedom: Virginia's Black Church's Role in the Rise of Christian Consciousness

Echoed throughout the eighteenth and early nineteenth centuries is the profound truth that a revolution begins in the spirit. Noted in these eras are changes that started in the hearts and minds of people whose desire for a societal shift was led by an inner awakening that then charged the oppressed to demand social change. Ordained as God's change agents, free Black people were among those in their church communities to guide the messaging around the spiritual values that addressed the concerns of those living on the periphery of mainstream society. This is where God's revolutionizing spirit manifested through movements that contributed to the revival of congregations and communities. Theologian J. Deotis Roberts considers the Black church to be a creation of the revolutionary spirit that functions through its institution and community. The religious scholar Wayne Croft describes the Black church as the only remaining institution that was "birthed from slavery and nurtured in the bosom of social protest." In other words, the church and its community have been energized by the Holy Spirit, which ushers in an observable change that has inspired congregants to shout "Hallelujah!" and "Amen!" along with other affirming expressions, through a call and response experience that reflects their gratitude for Christ who made himself accessible and present during moments of praise and worship.[24]

In a time when racism was a core societal problem (as it still is today), Black congregants who were free were highly aware of the importance of embodying a revolutionary spirit. Those who sought change during the early nineteenth century strategized outreach programs that spoke to Black people's concerns in ways that continued to raise their consciousness in the Christian tradition. This has been the testimony of some of the Commonwealth's places of worship, including two of its historical Black churches.[25]

Evidence of the rise of Christian consciousness was observed in the historic efforts of the First Baptist Church of Petersburg and Gillfield Baptist Church in Petersburg—a city known for having the highest number of free Black residents in Virginia. The community's ability to stand strong, as they faced arson attacks at their sanctuaries by white supremacists who feared Black activism, was a testimony to their revolutionary spirit. Before the separation of its integrated congregation in 1800, First Baptist Church underwent three name changes while continuing to raise the community's Christian consciousness. First Baptist operated on multiple sites at the plantations in Prince George and Lunenburg counties. For centuries, it also operated within less than a mile from its neighboring house of worship, Gillfield Baptist. Both congregations included free people who considered the Petersburg community's spiritual development and academic, social, and economic growth to be their top priorities.[26]

Rev. Henry Williams (1831–1900), frontispiece image in *A Sketch of the Life of Rev. Henry Williams, D.D., Late Pastor of the Gilfield [sic] Baptist Church*, by William H. Johnson (Petersburg, Va.: Fenn & Owen, 1901). *VMHC*

Gillfield Baptist Church has long been known for its service-minded leaders. Reverend Henry Williams, Pastor Emeritus, was considered an enthusiastic leader of community action. As a part of the former pastor's service, which started before the end of the Civil War and continued until his death in 1900, he founded Gillfield's Sabbath School, in which members of the church would receive spiritual teachings together with an academic education. Williams also worked beyond the church's walls to ensure that the city of Petersburg understood the need to educate all its citizens. Out of concern for Petersburg's teachers' salaries, he campaigned for equal pay among Black teachers and their white counterparts. Known as a vigilant spirit who was determined to do his part in moving the Commonwealth of Virginia forward, Williams sought to advance the city's community without tolerance for any form of societal setback. This level of passion, as also exhibited by other church leaders, was one of many reasons why Black people in the eighteenth and early nineteenth centuries considered their churches to be spiritual safe havens that shielded them from discrimination. Grounded in the mission of divine service, First Baptist Church of Petersburg and Gillfield Baptist Church have continued the tradition of producing leaders and change agents for Christ, as inspired by founding members of their churches who laid the groundwork for the revolution of Black freedom during the eighteenth and early nineteenth centuries.[27]

Holding a profound place in Virginia's history, Black churches became the heart of change through free Black leaders and congregants who addressed the social, economic, and political concerns of marginalized communities in order to make life bearable for the oppressed. The Commonwealth's requirement for white ministers to supervise Black churches did not stifle the revolutionary influences of free Black ministers and congregants who were active in the community. In effect, those who sought religious autonomy from the white churches established places of worship that also served as schools and political gathering places. As early as the 1830s, such churches served as an "ark of safety" that carried both free and enslaved Black people through storms of oppression by providing stalwart community support. These institutions continued to be a source of strength in serving as benevolent organizations that assisted people in social and economic distress.[28]

Most Black congregants during the early nineteenth century were Baptist; however, Presbyterian, Catholic, African American Episcopal, and African American Episcopal Zion churches were later erected. These buildings, which were some of the largest structures in many of Virginia's regions, symbolized the central roles they played in the lives of oppressed communities. After the Revolutionary War, the denominations licensed Black ministers and free preachers who were literate and educated, and often assumed community leadership roles. Their representation and efforts were most important to recently manumitted congregants who were increasing their literacy.[29]

Among the notable leaders and spiritual revolutionists who valued the fusion of religion, culture, and education in the consciousness-raising process that was occurring in the Black community was Mary Smith Kelsey Peake. Born in Norfolk, Virginia, in 1823, the educator was the daughter of a free Black mother and a white Englishman or Frenchman, who were unable to legally marry under the laws of the Commonwealth. Peake's mother sent her to live with relatives in the city of Alexandria, where she was educated by a white Englishman at First Baptist Colored Church (later known as Alfred Street Baptist Church). While there, she lived in a house owned by Rollins Fowle, a white man who purchased enslaved people at risk of being sold to cruel owners. Fowle granted freedom to the people he purchased and helped them to establish businesses.[30]

Mary Smith Kelsey Peake (1823–1862), about 1860, photograph. *Courtesy of Hampton University Archives*

Toward the end of the 1830s, Peake returned to her mother's residence in Norfolk with strong religious convictions that led her to join the First Baptist Church on Bute Street. In 1847, Peake and her mother established residence in Hampton, where Peake's stepfather, Thompson Walker, was an enslaved foreman of a local plantation and a founder of Zion Baptist Church, the city's second oldest Black church. To support herself, Peake became a successful seamstress, and she also began to teach free and enslaved Blacks of all ages, including her stepfather. After Nat Turner's Rebellion in 1831, Virginia legislators had passed a law to close all schools to free Black people and to forbid members of the enslaved community from receiving an education. Apparently, however, even in a time when conducting schools for Black Americans was outlawed, local white authorities did not disrupt Peake's school.

In 1851, she married Thomas D. Peake, a formerly enslaved merchant mariner who could pass for white. The Peakes became one of the most prominent families in Hampton, seeking to raise the Christian consciousness of oppressed people, despite risking their own lives and freedom as they educated Black people who sought liberation. Their home served as a meeting place for people who engaged in Christian ministry. Fueled by a revolutionary spirit, Mary Smith Kelsey Peake's sacrifices for the Black community led her into a future that involved teaching for the American Missionary Association and providing instruction for six newly freed Black people near Fort Monroe on the present grounds of Hampton University. Peake taught her classes there underneath a large oak tree—later known as the Emancipation Oak Tree. This became the location where the Hampton community attended one of the first public readings of President Abraham Lincoln's Emancipation Proclamation in the South.

As her classes grew to more than fifty students, including her daughter, the school moved to a new location (near Chesapeake Female Seminary), where Peake taught children reading, writing, math, and the Bible. She also incorporated the singing of hymns into the curriculum. The blend of spiritual and secular education that was provided in Peake's curriculum might be indicative of her intentions to provide a holistic educational experience to people in an imbalanced world with lopsided norms. Her story presents opportunities for understanding how many free Black people with Christian convictions did all that they could (with the resources they had) to revolutionize freedom by raising the spiritual consciousness of a vulnerable population of people who were driven by their struggles to someday become influential agents of change.[31]

The narratives of free Black people serve as meaningful testaments to the quest for liberty, justice, and equality as viewed through their faith. The stories featured in this chapter highlight the fortitude and agency of individuals who forged communities, established churches, and pursued emancipation for themselves and others, despite living through systemic oppression. The valuable insights into the intersection of faith and social justice reflect the roles of free Black people through instructive testaments of resilience. Their lives show that the rise of Christian consciousness in the eighteenth through early nineteenth centuries among free Black people is a complex history, with an integration of spiritual beliefs, preserved elements of African culture, and adaptation to a new world in which they confronted immense pain. The examination of their experiences uncovers unimaginable suffering among an "un/bound" people who lived in parallel and in solidarity with those who were enslaved. As the stories of Virginia's free Black people have been called from the corners of society, we are reminded to keep our faith at the core of our existence and to remain vigilant, engaged, responsive, and informed, as we affirm freedom as God's revolution and the citizens' responsibility.[32]

Chapter 3

Free Black People in Rural Virginia: Forms of Resistance

3

Free Black People in Rural Virginia: Forms of Resistance

Sabrina G. Watson

Virginia had one of the largest populations of free Black Americans in the antebellum South. In 1860, the population in Virginia numbered approximately 58,000. Free Black life in the South is not a new subject of scholarly inquiry. But conventional histories often sideline it, and in K-12 education it is rarely included. This is particularly so with regards to the ways in which free Black people resisted repression from the state and discrimination from broader white American society. White southerners had contradictory views toward Black Americans, framing them as submissive, docile, and suited for enslavement, while also fearing their capacity for violence because of incidents like Gabriel's Rebellion in 1800 and Nat Turner's Rebellion in 1831.

This perception ignores the intricate dynamics of slavery, Black agency, and the complexity of race relations in Virginia. African Americans, whether free or enslaved, found many ways to resist oppression and the limitations placed upon them by white Virginians in the colonial, early republic, and antebellum periods. Resistance to slavery could include breaking tools, working slowly, feigning sickness, escaping from one's enslaver, and participating in insurrection. Meanwhile, free Black Virginians' resistance to a state and society that sought to limit their freedoms often involved refusing to answer court summons, remaining in Virginia despite a law requiring them to leave, or leaving the Commonwealth to pursue other opportunities for freedom elsewhere. Analysis of court documents and registers of free Black people can spotlight how free Black persons at the county level responded to the demands of the state as it sought to control and surveil a growing free Black population in Virginia.

Free Black Virginians like Esther Evans, Joe Watson, and Eliza Harris in Accomack and Isle of Wight counties were often summoned to their respective county courts so that their free status could be investigated. And yet, they often chose not to appear at court when summoned. Free Black Virginians defied the state by remaining in the Commonwealth, despite the 1806 law requiring people freed from slavery to leave the state within a year or face re-enslavement. This essay will focus on several free African Americans who did not answer their court summons and who stayed in the state beyond the allowed twelve months. While we do not have access to letters, diaries, or other textual sources written by Evans, Watson, or Harris, we can learn about them through court documents produced in county clerk offices. These records have been made available through *Virginia Untold*, a Library of Virginia digital database initiative that also includes records from the Virginia Museum of History & Culture's *Unknown No Longer* project. *Virginia Untold* provides expanded access to records that help document the identities and experiences of free and enslaved Black people in Virginia.

The records relating to Evans, Watson, and Harris represent but a small sample of free Black individuals who defied state laws by rejecting their summons. The records from Accomack and Isle of Wight show how free Black individuals navigated state laws to remain in their county and state. Without further documentation relating to arrest, re-enslavement, or other court matters, it is apparent that despite their summons, white authorities often chose not to take further action. Ignoring these calls to court should be understood as a successful form of resistance on the part of free Black people. By remaining in the state and choosing not to answer court summons, free African Americans demonstrated their awareness of the law and any potential repercussions they might face, and were able to exert agency within its confines.

Scholarship on free Black people provides important context about their resistance to the courts. The Black historian Luther Porter Jackson, writing as early as the 1940s, examined free Black people, property ownership, and labor in the South, exploring their aspirations and ability to own land in Virginia. In so doing, Jackson was one of the first historians to explain how free Black men came to own land in Virginia by tracing numbers of free Black people in the state, where they owned land, and the demand for their labor in counties that relied heavily on agriculture as part of their economies. Even as white politicians and government officials placed greater legal constraints upon free Black people between 1830 and 1860, access to their labor could be more important to their white counterparts than upholding state laws that discriminated against them. Thus, free Blacks not only defied laws but were in turn supported by their white neighbors who might ignore the requirement to enforce them. Many African Americans defined freedom by their ability to own property. This was a way for free Black people to support themselves financially and increase generational wealth by having something to pass on to their children to secure a better future for them.[1]

Ira Berlin's 1972 book, *Slaves Without Masters*, asserts as its central point that free African Americans were ultimately less than free. In relation to the growing free Black population in Virginia, Berlin notes that, in the American Revolution, both Loyalists and Patriots offered a pathway to freedom for African Americans that helped the overall growth of Virginia's free Black population. But Berlin and others more often attribute growth to the Baptist, Methodist, and other churches, whose members struggled with the spiritual and moral consequences of enslaving others. After the Revolution, the number of manumissions grew significantly in the state of Virginia. White Virginians established many of the repressive laws that concerned free Black people in response to this burgeoning population, and intensified the process in response to flashpoints of active, violent resistance by Black people not only in Virginia but across the Atlantic World. These included domestic incidents like Gabriel's Rebellion and Nat Turner's Rebellion, as well as violence abroad, notably the Haitian Revolution. White anxiety centered around the free Black community's perceived capacity for violence and led to initiatives to stymy the growth of the population and to encourage the removal of individuals from the state. However, as indicated by rural, city and county records following the 1806 expulsion law, enforcement of the policy across many municipalities was challenging or limited.[2]

Historians writing about free African Americans during the antebellum period have examined the various ways individuals resisted slavery, racism, and white supremacy, illuminating our understanding of their lives, the work they completed, and their response to laws and social norms that oppressed them. A single free Black community does not exemplify all in Virginia, and one must be attentive to time, place, and how white Virginians coexisted with their free Black neighbors. Moreover, there are still many unknowns due to issues of literacy and education among free Black populations as well as the role of archives in overlooking source material created by free Black people. The historical record can depict these often-silenced figures as a monolithic group instead of as complex individuals with varied experiences.

Several state laws passed in antebellum Virginia specifically targeted free Black people with the intention of ensuring their subservience and second-class status, while maintaining the primacy of slavery to the state's economic and social systems. Many free Black people living in rural areas moved around and even left the state as they pursued personal and economic opportunities, whether they avoided the expulsion law or chose to leave on their own terms. Of course, court records and their role in underpinning much of the research on free Black people in Virginia still privilege white perspectives and render Black individuals voiceless in the telling of their own stories.

Virginia was a leader in the efforts to codify African slavery between 1660 and 1705 among the British colonies, solidifying the status of enslaved people of African descent and differentiating this status from indentured servitude as undertaken by white colonists. Similarly, lawmakers worked to prevent free Blacks from gaining fuller rights as residents of the colony. By 1723, the

ACT XII.

Negro womens children to serve according to the condition of the mother. (a)

WHEREAS some doubts have arrisen whether children got by any Englishman upon a negro woman should be slave or ffree, *Be it therefore enacted and declared by this present grand assembly,* that all children borne in this country shalbe held bond or free only according to the condition of the mother, *And* that if any christian shall committ ffornication with a negro man or woman, hee or shee soe offending shall pay double the ffines imposed by the former act.

"Act XII. Negro womens children to serve according to the condition of the mother," 1662, from *The Statutes at Large; Being a Collection of All the Laws of Virginia . . .* , by William Waller Hening (14 vols.: New York: R. & W. & G. Bartow, 1823), 2:170. *VMHC*

Lord Dunmore's Proclamation, November 7, 1775, broadside.
Courtesy of the Library of Virginia

colonial government had curtailed the rights of free Black people by denying them votes and prohibiting them from carrying weapons. Such laws worked to gradually foster racial, social, and political divisions within Virginia. After the founding of the United States and in response to the growing number of free Black people, the General Assembly intensified the process of repressive and reactionary lawmaking. They worked to reinforce earlier laws, removed inconsistencies, and prevented free Black Virginians from enjoying the new liberties promised by the Revolution. White elites instead required them to follow new regulations to ensure their subordination. In 1793, changes in state law prevented free Black people from other states from moving into the Commonwealth.[3]

To discourage growth of the free Black population, the state passed legislation requiring that free people register with a local county clerk. These clerks would record the individual's name, sex, color, age, stature, any identifying marks, and how they had achieved their freedom. Through this registration process, the state built a picture of the free Black population and could track individuals at the county level. In 1803, Virginia updated a law dating from the 1790s requiring that clerks keep track of the free Black people in their respective counties. The assembly followed this with a draconian law three years later that allowed for the enslavement of free Blacks remaining in the state after one year:

> *And be it further enacted*, That if any slave hereafter emancipated shall remain within this commonwealth more than twelve months after his or her right to freedom shall have accrued, he or she shall forfeit all such right, and may be apprehended and sold by the overseers of the poor of any county or corporation in which he or she shall be found, for the benefit of the poor of such county or corporation.[4]

By His Excellency the Right Honorable JOHN Earl of DUNMORE, His MAJESTY's Lieutenant and Governor General of the Colony and Dominion of VIRGINIA, and Vice Admiral of the same.

A PROCLAMATION.

AS I have ever entertained Hopes that an Accommodation might have taken Place between GREAT-BRITAIN and this Colony, without being compelled by my Duty to this most disagreeable but now absolutely necessary Step, rendered so by a Body of armed Men unlawfully assembled, firing on His MAJESTY's Tenders, and the formation of an Army, and that Army now on their March to attack His MAJESTY's Troops and destroy the well disposed Subjects of this Colony. To defeat such treasonable Purposes, and that all such Traitors, and their Abettors, may be brought to Justice, and that the Peace, and good Order of this Colony may be again restored, which the ordinary Course of the Civil Law is unable to effect; I have thought fit to issue this my Proclamation, hereby declaring, that until the aforesaid good Purposes can be obtained, I do in Virtue of the Power and Authority to ME given, by His MAJESTY, determine to execute Martial Law, and cause the same to be executed throughout this Colony: and to the end that Peace and good Order may the sooner be effected, I do require every Person capable of bearing Arms, to resort to His MAJESTY's STANDARD, or be looked upon as Traitors to His MAJESTY's Crown and Government, and thereby become liable to the Penalty the Law inflicts upon such Offences; such as forfeiture of Life, confiscation of Lands, &c. &c. And I do hereby further declare all indented Servants, Negroes, or others, (appertaining to Rebels,) free that are able and willing to bear Arms, they joining His MAJESTY's Troops as soon as may be, for the more speedily reducing this Colony to a proper Sense of their Duty, to His MAJESTY's Crown and Dignity. I do further order, and require, all His MAJESTY's Leige Subjects, to retain their Quitrents, or any other Taxes due or that may become due, in their own Custody, till such Time as Peace may be again restored to this at present most unhappy Country, or demanded of them for their former salutary Purposes, by Officers properly authorised to receive the same.

GIVEN under my Hand on board the Ship WILLIAM, off NORFOLK, the 7th Day of NOVEMBER, in the SIXTEENTH Year of His MAJESTY's Reign.

DUNMORE.

(GOD save the KING.)

There were several counties which continued to have substantial Black populations that maintained their free status in Virginia despite the law. The process of upholding the law and the new requirement of registering free Black people at the county level was problematic and inefficient. Free Black residents were liable to manipulate the system, with implications for enslaved communities. Some free individuals forged their papers and others, claiming that they had lost their papers, applied for new certificates, then passed these onto enslaved people for their own use. The forging and exchange of free papers was a form of resistance that saw both free and enslaved Black Virginians cooperate to allow for greater movement around the state.[5]

White authorities extended control over the free Black population at the local level. But as individuals were summoned to confront courts and officials, there was often little to no follow-up unless the person in question actually presented themselves at court to face their charges. Accomack County court papers illustrate several instances in which free Black residents like Joe Watson, Esther Evans, and Eliza Harris avoided charges by refusing or neglecting to appear in court. Whether ultimately determined by a rejection of the summons on the part of Black individuals or by white officials' inability to apprehend (either because they did not have the willingness or resources, or because the individual had temporarily absconded from the area), it is apparent that the dictates of the state were not always complied with at the local level.

The presence of a growing free Black population exacerbated white fears of slave rebellions in antebellum Virginia, especially among the planter class. Southern whites were acutely aware of the role that free people of color had played in both bringing about and maintaining the Haitian Revolution, and they held serious concerns about restlessness among Virginia's own growing free Black population. In Henrico County, Gabriel's Rebellion—a planned insurrection of enslaved people that whites stopped before its execution—

Smithfield Court House, Smithfield, Isle of Wight County, Va., Frances Benjamin Johnston, about 1933. *Library of Congress*

"Nat Turner & his confederates in conference," from *History of American Conspiracies*, by Orville J. Victor (New York: James D. Torrey, 1863). *Schomburg Center for Research in Black Culture, The New York Public Library, 1229308*

List of Free Negroes in St. Geo's. Parish for the year 1851, February 1, 1851, *Virginia Untold: The African American Narrative Digital Collection*. *Library of Virginia (1138011_0002_0002_0001)*

A Complete List of all Free Negroes over twelve Years of age, in the District of John J. Blackstone, Commissioner of the Revenue for the Parish of Saint George, in the County of Accomack and State of Virginia, On the first day of February A. D. 1851. –

Names of Free Negroes over twelve Years of age.	Sexes	Ages	Trade or Occupation	Names of Free Negroes.	Sexes	Ages	Trade or Occupation
Tom Allen	Male	30	Laborer	John Ames	Male	20	Feed hand
Danl. Allen	"	45	"	Henry Ames	"	18	"
Nelson Ashby	"	27	"	Vernetta Ames	F.	14	"
Smith Ames	"	19	"	Chs. Allen	M.	20	"
Sarah Ashby	F.	17	"	Levin Allen	"	20	"
Joice Ashby	"	23	"	Sarah Ames	F.	21	"
Esther Ashby	"	21	"				
Mary Allen	"	22	"				
Tabby Allen	"	50	Cook	B.			
Tamor Ashby	"	45	"	Robin Brickhouse			
Ezer Allen	Male	28	Field hand	John Beckett	Male	21	Laborer
Robert Allen	"	26	"	Levin Bagly	"	23	"
Jim Allen	"	20	"	Jinny Beckett	F.	28	"
John Ames	"	32	"	Edmd. Burton	M.	22	"
Jesse Ames	"	38	Laborer	Arthur Bagly	"	24	"
Jim Ashby	"	27	"	Mary Burton	F.	19	"
Edmd. Ashby	"	29	"	Joshua Beckett	Male	22	"
Jim Ames	"	19	"	Wm. Beckett	"	25	"
Matilda Ames	F.	65	Spinner	Jim Bevans	"	31	"
George Ames	Male	20	Sailor	Wm. Bevans	"	24	"
Saml. Ames	"	23	"	Ailsey Bevans	F.	22	"
Esther Ames	F.	47	Cook	George Bagly	Male	35	Farm hand
Frank Ames	Male	65	Laborer	Leah Burton	F.	50	Cook
Sheppard Ames	"	32	"	Harriet Burton	"	25	Laborer
Kasey Ames	F.	48	Spinner	Mary Burton	"	48	"
Edmd. Ames	Male	26	Sailor	Litt Bagly	Male	20	"
Levin Ames	"	24	"	Mary Bundick	F.	28	"

50

caused anxiety among plantation owners. White authorities executed Gabriel and his associates, and they changed and reinforced laws to further repress both the free and enslaved populations. For example, one law called for more patrols made up of white citizens to surveil and control Black Virginians. James Monroe, then the governor of Virginia, had personally requested it. In 1831, following Nat Turner's Rebellion, the legislature passed another wave of repressive laws. One act required local county clerks to document those who they believed had remained in Virginia despite the expulsion law:

> *Be it further enacted*, That it shall be the duty of all commissioners of the public revenue, once in every year, to present to the grand juries of the several courts aforesaid, a list of all free negroes and mulattoes, who, in the opinion of such commissioners, may have remained within the commonwealth, contrary to law, upwards of twelve months from the time of their emancipation.

Free Black people remained in Virginia longer than the allotted twelve months, and there are few instances demonstrating that local officials followed up on the identification of these individuals and enforced their removal. This was particularly so in rural counties.[6]

County court records from Accomack and Isle of Wight indicate that free Black people stayed in their local areas and petitioned to remain. Historian Ellen Eslinger explored the lack of effort by white Virginians to enforce the laws in a study of Rockbridge and Augusta counties. By examining residency laws, Eslinger points toward public apathy, a preprofessional police force unable to enforce laws efficiently, protective white patrons who stepped in to defend their Black neighbors, and direct Black resistance. Often, it was some combination of these factors. Without personal and private documents that might illuminate the interior worlds of free Black Virginians, we lose an opportunity to better understand the motives as to why they chose not to obey the laws. However, the population of free African Americans in Rockbridge and Augusta counties was far smaller than those found in Accomack and Isle of Wight counties. Thus, white citizens' lack of consistency in enforcing the laws perhaps points to a lack of concern over these relatively small free Black communities. In those cases where the law required free African Americans to leave, they had the opportunity to petition local courts and offer a justification for their remaining in Virginia.[7]

As laws restricting free Black people increased through the antebellum period, there was a direct correlation in the increase in the number of white officials calling free Black people into court. But these officials appear to have taken little direct action. Even when authorities denied a petition to remain by a free Black resident, many chose to stay and simply submitted another request.[8]

Many free Black people continued to violate the expulsion law despite efforts by white lawmakers to improve the system of removal in 1831. A consideration of what the Virginia laws were and how the free Black residents responded allows one to better understand the acts of resistance occurring in Accomack and Isle of Wight counties, demonstrating the gulf between laws as presented in theory and as executed in practice. In fact, free Black people would remain in a state committed to their repression even during flashpoints of white supremacist lawmaking in the aftermath of overt, violent acts of Black resistance.[9]

Accomack County had the largest free Black population in Virginia in 1860. The 4,380 Black residents in the county formed 7.5 percent of the free Black population in the state. It was also the Commonwealth's oldest free Black enclave. As in other places, authorities regularly summoned free Black residents of Accomack for violating state law requiring them to leave Virginia. One such individual was Esther Evans. Evans received manumission in 1806, the same year that the state passed the expulsion law. Strikingly, authorities summoned Evans in 1851 for remaining in the state: she had continued to live in Virginia for approximately forty-four years after she was meant to leave. Others, like Rachel Major, Sharack Watson, Joe Watson, Hannah Wise, and Isaac Revell, remained in the state, and were summoned to court to offer explanations as to why they had remained for longer than the year allotted to them.[10]

Of the above individuals, it is apparent that only Joe Watson, who had been manumitted by his enslaver Arthur Watson in the latter's will in 1819, was summoned to the court multiple times. Watson's summons of 1829 read, in part:

> That Joe Watson, free negro, of the parish of Accomack, in the County of Accomack aforesaid, labourer, was on the 14th day of April A.D. 1819

a slave of a certain Arthur Watson, late of the parish and county aforesaid; that afterwards and since the first day of May A.D. 1806, viz, on the same 14th day of April A.D. 1819 aforesaid, the said Arthur Watson, by his last Will and testament, then duly made and published, emancipated and set free the said Joe Watson; that afterwards viz on the 28th day of June A.D. 1819, the said Arthur Watson departed this life, leaving the said Will in full force and unrevoked, and afterwards, viz. on the same day and year last aforesaid the said last will and testament of the said Arthur Watson was duly proved and admitted to the County Court of aforesaid.[11]

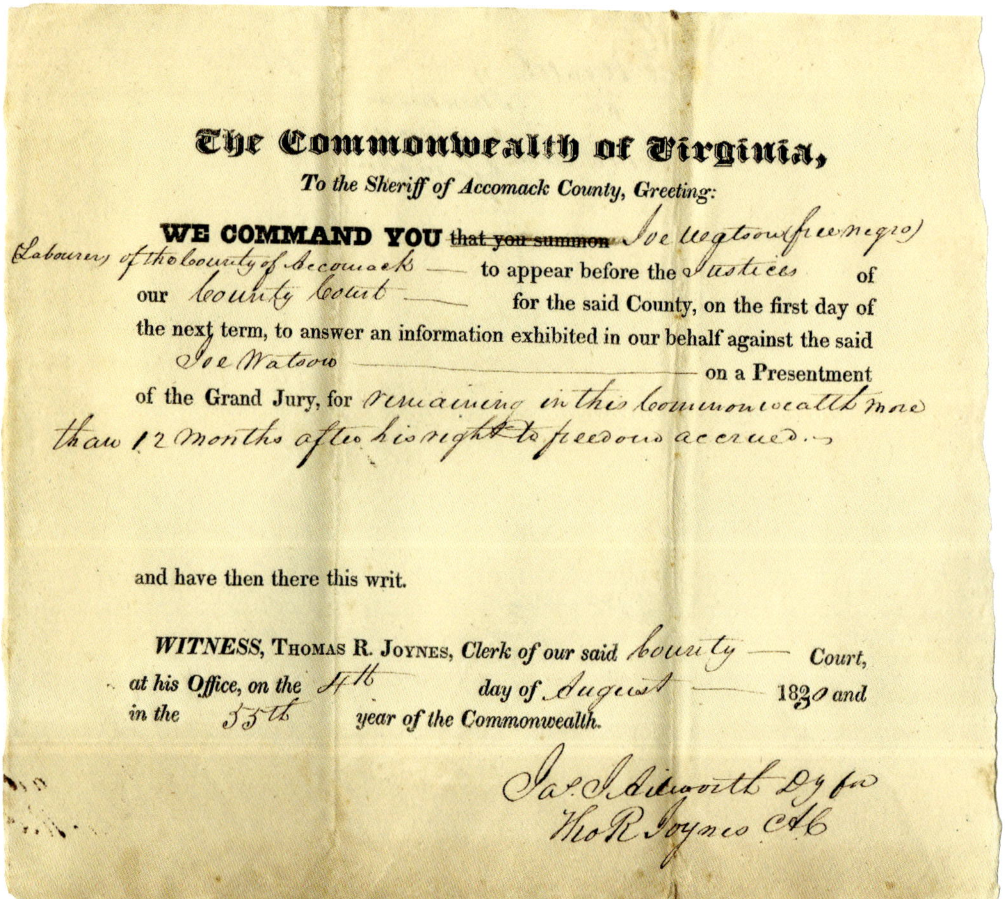

The Commonwealth of Virginia,

To the Sheriff of Accomack County, Greeting:

WE COMMAND YOU ~~that you summon~~ Joe Watson (free negro) Labourer of the County of Accomack to appear before the Justices of our County Court for the said County, on the first day of the next term, to answer an information exhibited in our behalf against the said Joe Watson on a Presentment of the Grand Jury, for remaining in this Commonwealth more than 12 months after his right to freedom accrued.

and have then there this writ.

WITNESS, Thomas R. Joynes, *Clerk of our said* County *Court, at his Office, on the* 4th *day of* August 1830 *and in the* 55th *year of the Commonwealth.*

Jas. S. Ailworth Dy for
Tho R Joynes CAC

Joe Watson, Commonwealth Cause, August 4, 1830, *Virginia Untold: The African American Narrative Digital Collection*. *Library of Virginia (7594199_0004_0025_0001)*

Joe Watson was a free Black laborer working in the county long after his manumission date. In 1824, Accomack County's register of free Black people listed him. In March 1826, county officials also included him in a record of "runaway slaves" and noted that he was imprisoned in Accomack County. But, by 1830, the court again summoned him for remaining:

> We command you Joe Watson (free negro) (Labourer) of the County of Accomack to appear before the Justices of our County Court for the said County, on the first day of the next term, to answer an information exhibited in our behalf against the said Joe Watson on a Presentment of the Grand Jury, for remaining in this Commonwealth more than 12 months after his right to freedom accrued.[12]

Later, in 1851, records show Watson on a list of free people who owed taxes. Watson owed $15.50, a notable sum in the period. But aside from a temporary imprisonment and multiple court summons, authorities did not remove Watson from the state, despite his having stayed there for decades. Did a need for labor in the county trump state law? Virginia's agricultural economy depended enough upon Black labor, and elite and middling white Virginians regularly supplemented enslaved workforces with the labor of free Black Virginians.[13]

But it was not just laboring Black men like Watson who were able to remain. Esther Evans was summoned to court in 1851 for staying in the state for more than forty years after she had been required to leave:

> We command you that you summon Esther Evans (f.n.) [free negro] to appear before the Justices of our County Court for the said County, on the first day of the next November term, to shew cause why an information should not be filed against her, upon a Presentment of the Grand Jury, made against her in the said Court, for remaining in this Commonwealth, twelve months after her right to freedom had accrued, and have then and there this writ.

Evans was manumitted in 1806. But research within the other available online documents, such as tax records or petitions to remain, do not reflect any form of follow-up from the county officials.[14]

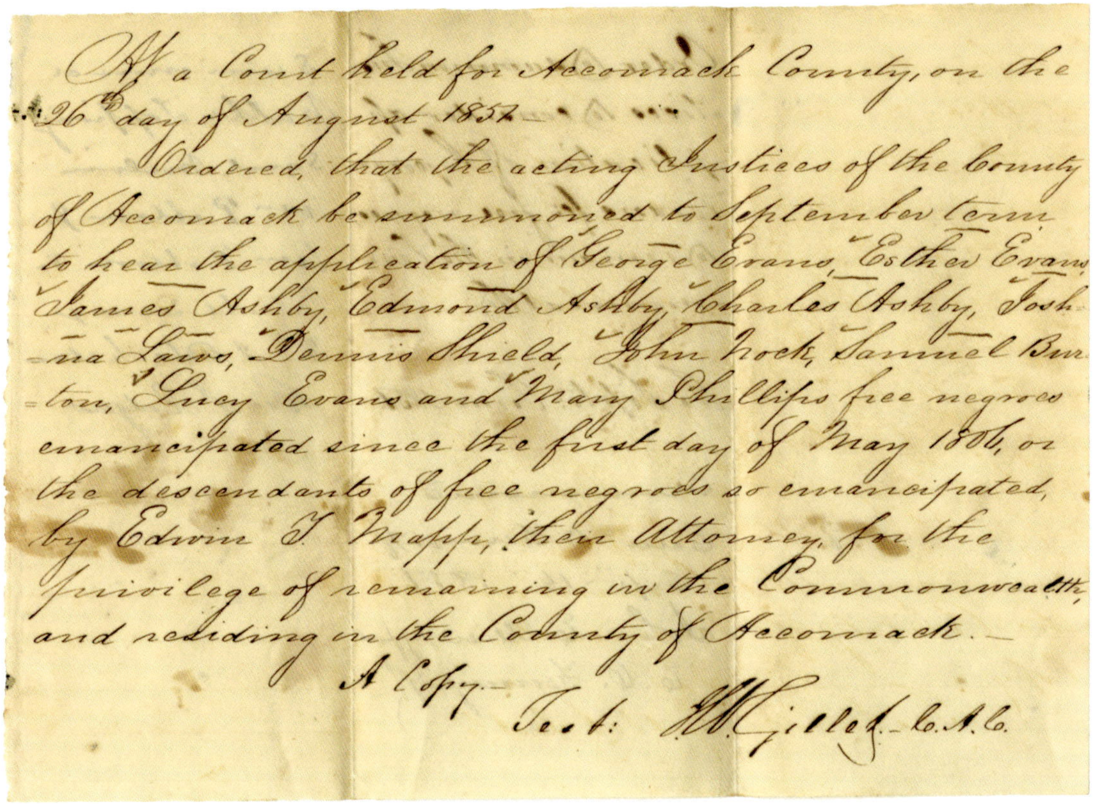

At a Court held for Accomack County, on the 26th day of August 1851 —

Ordered, that the acting Justices of the County of Accomack be summoned to September term to hear the application of George Evans, Esther Evans, James Ashby, Edmond Ashby, Charles Ashby, Joshua Laws, Dennis Shield, John Rock, Samuel Burton, Lucy Evans and Mary Phillips free negroes emancipated since the first day of May 1806, or the descendants of free negroes so emancipated, by Edwin T. Mapp, their Attorney, for the privilege of remaining in the Commonwealth, and residing in the County of Accomack.—

A Copy.—

Test: [illegible] C.A.C.

Esther Evans, Petition to Remain in the Commonwealth, August 26, 1851, *Virginia Untold: The African American Narrative Digital Collection*. *Library of Virginia (1138011_0014_0008_0001)*

Another example of a free Black resident of the county who did not present himself at court is Harry Tunnell. Freed in May 1806, Tunnell was summoned to court by authorities in 1836, 1842, 1848, 1849, and four times in 1850:

> We command you, as we have heretofore commanded you that you do not omit for any liberty in your bailiwick, but that you take Harry Tunnell (fn) late of the Parish of Accomack in the County aforesaid if he be found within the same, and him safely keep, so that you have his body, before the Justices of our County Court for the said County of Accomack at the court-house thereof on the 1st day of the next August Term of the said Court, to answer us of a certain Misdemeanor whereof he stands charged. And have then there this writ.[15]

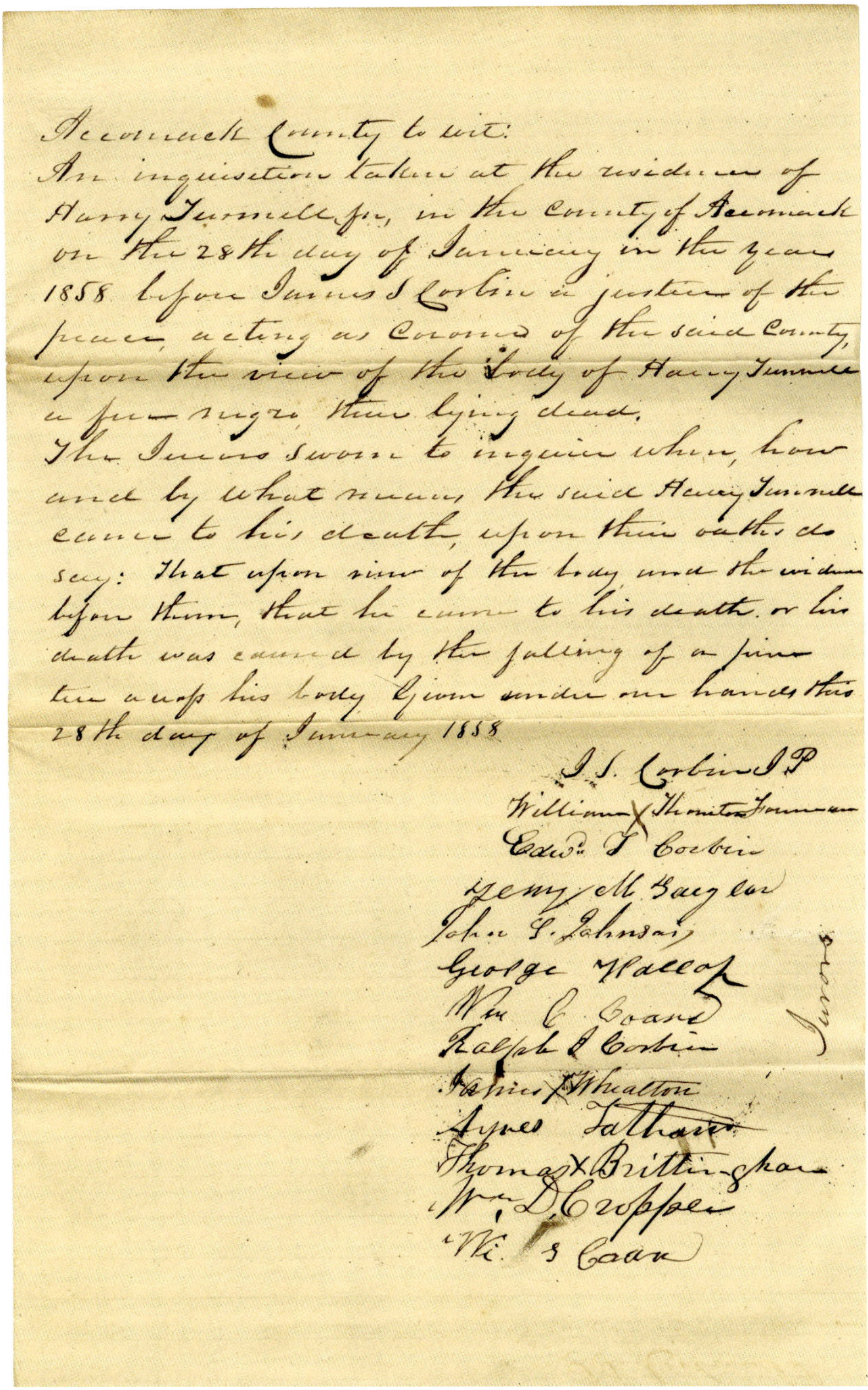

Accomack County to wit:
An inquisition taken at the residence of Harry Tunnell Jr, in the County of Accomack on the 28th day of January in the year 1858 before James J Corbin a justice of the peace, acting as Coroner of the said County, upon the view of the body of Harry Tunnell a free negro there lying dead.
The Jurors sworn to inquire when, how and by what means the said Harry Tunnell came to his death, upon their oaths do say: That upon view of the body and the evidence before them, that he came to his death or his death was caused by the falling of a pine tree across his body Given under our hands this 28th day of January 1858

J. J. Corbin J.P.
William X Thornton Foreman
Edwd. J. Corbin
Henry M. Baylor
John S. Johnson
George Walloss
Wm C. Coard
Ralph J Corbin
James X Wheatton
Ayres Latham
Thomas X Brittingham
Wm D. Cropper
Wm S Caan
Jurors

Harry Tunnell, Coroner's Inquisition, January 28, 1858, *Virginia Untold: The African American Narrative Digital Collection*. *Library of Virginia (7588285_0003_0024_0001)*

Richard Ligon, Bond for the Purchase and Removal of Hembry and Others (including Jack Harden), October 23, 1827, *Virginia Untold: The African American Narrative Digital Collection*. Library of Virginia (7430184_0009_0007_0001)

These notes imply that Tunnell could not be found. Whether through Tunnell's own efforts to knowingly avoid the court and the officials employed there, or by lackluster efforts on the part of authorities who sought to check bureaucratic boxes rather than fully enforce the law, Tunnell was able to remain in Virginia despite the requirement that he leave.

In 1860, 1,370 free Black people called Isle of Wight County home. Here, William Lightfoot, Elizabeth Johnson, Wiley Clary, Martha Jones, Zeney or Zena Davis, Joseph Holloway, Jack (no surname), Jack Harden, Nancy Green, Louisa Shepperd, Louis Hardy, and Eliza or Lizzy Harris were all summoned for remaining in the state, but officials dealt no apparent further consequences after summoning the men and women. Isle of Wight County had a smaller free Black population compared to Accomack County, pointing toward white indifference to their free Black neighbors.[16]

In the existent records for Isle of Wight, there are several individuals whom officials repeatedly summoned and who subsequently either chose not to appear in court or simply benefitted from the county's inability or unwillingness to enforce the law. Eliza Harris, or Lizzy Harris, appears as a free woman of color in 1806, freed by her owner, Josiah M. Jordan. The courts summoned Harris in 1838 and 1839 for remaining in the state. But they dismissed her charges in 1839, and no other historical documents are available with regards to her. On the other hand, Jack Harden was called into court for trying to avoid a summons in 1826, and was then tried for grand larceny.[17]

A comparison of Accomack and Isle of Wight counties shows similarities regarding each locale's approach to upholding state laws regarding free Black people. It is apparent that the difficulties in enforcing these laws, whether due to Black resistance or white disinterest in carrying out the removal of Black persons, were commonplace. Oftentimes, it appears as though local authorities registered free Black people and carried out summons in accordance with the

Know all men by these presents that we Richard Ligon Richard Ligon Jr. Daniel Ligon Archibald Ligon and Alfred Wood are held and firmly bound unto Wm B Giles Governor or chief Magistrate of the commonwealth of Virginia and to his successors in Office in the sum of Twenty four Thousand Nine hundred and Sixty Dollars to be paid to the said William B Giles and to his successors in Office for the use of the Literary fund to which payment well and truly to be made we bind ourselves, our heirs Executors Administrators and Assigns firmly by these presents Sealed with our Seals and dated this 23rd day of October Eighteen hundred and Twenty Seven.

The Condition of the above obligation is such that whereas the Executive pursuant to the powers vested in them by an act of the General Assembly passed the 2d day of March 1819, entitled "An Act to reduce into one the several acts Concerning slaves free negroes and mulattoes" have sold to Richard Ligon the following slaves under sentence of death for the commission of the following crimes, to Wit: Hembry Sentensed by the Court of Louisa for felony: Ann by the Court of Spottsylvania for setting fire to a Barn: George Henry by the Court of Hustings of Richmond for felony: Jack Harden by the Court of Isle of Wight for grand larceny: Robert by the Court of Fauquier for an assault upon a white man: John by the Court of Louisa for an assault: Stephen by the Court of King George for horse stealing: Caleb by the Court of Amherst for burglary: George by the Court of Hanover for an assault: Richard Roberts by the Court of Stafford for manslaughter: Smith by the Court of Prince Edward for burglary: James by the Court of Montgomery for an attempt to commit a rape on a white woman: Jerry by the Court of Caroline for an attempt to administer poison: Wm Wingfield by the Court of Prince William for murder: James by the Court of Greenbrier for horse stealing and Albert by the same Court for the same offence: Harrison by the Court of Dinwiddie for felony: Richard by the Court of Fauquier for an assault with intent to kill: Arther by the Court of Northampton for burglary: Robin and Little Stephen by the Court of Lunenburg for murder: Toby by the Court of Culpeper for burglary: Reuben by the Court of Essex for forgery: Jack by the Court of Cumberland for burglary: Mathew by the Court of King George for an assault: Nelson by the Court of Lunenburg for murder: Bob and Will by the Court of York for burglary: Lewis and Robert by the Court of Fauquier for burglary: James and Buckner by the Court of Culpeper for horse stealing: Moses by the Court of Southampton for an assault: Henry by the Court of Mathews for an assault upon a white woman. Also the following free persons of color who have been sentensed to be sold as slaves and transported and banished beyond the limits of the United States under an act of the General Assembly passed 21st February 1823 intitled "An Act further to amend the penal laws of this commonwealth – To Wit David Denson by the Court of Nansemond for malicious stabbing: Mace Alexander by the Court of Loudon for larceny: Bill Butler by the same Court for the same offence and Miranda by the same Court for the murder of her child: Joseph Byrd by the Court of Surry for burglary: Walter Scott by the Court of Henrico for larceny: Lewis Bluesteel by the Court of Nansemond for assault and Robbery: Thomas Thompson by the Court of Lee for murder in the 2nd degree: Harold Smith by the Court of Halifax for felony: John Cambridge by the Court of Prince William for felony & burglary: Foster Batkins by the Court of New Kent for larceny: Henry Jumper by the Court of Hustings of Petersburg for larceny: Abram Wilson by the Court of Petersburg for feloniously and maliciously shooting: Claiborne Henderson by the Court of Dinwiddie for felony And Aaron Bridgewater by the Court of Petersburg for larceny.

Now if the said Richard Ligon shall well and faithfully Carry out of the United States all and every of the aforesaid Convicts so Sentensed for transportation as aforesaid according to the true intent and meaning of the before law but avoided following it to the point of organizing the removal or re-enslavement of these individuals.

Enforcing the day-to-day policies that sought to repress free Black men and women was difficult, too: officials would have been hard-pressed to verify the status of every Black person traveling in and through their county. Consistent enforcement of the law was problematic: larger populations of free Black people were difficult to record and control, and smaller populations like those in Rockbridge County were likely to be perceived as less of a threat to their white neighbors. Even so, when papers were issued to be able to identify free Black people among the larger enslaved population, free people could easily forge them, and many freed people moved far from where they had been manumitted, making it difficult for officials to verify their status. That free African Americans did not always follow the law and outright forged documents for others illustrates their awareness of the limits of white authority and their agency in resisting state power. This is not to argue that the state and broader white society did not exert a powerful and repressive influence over their lives, but that they navigated the courts using their knowledge of local systems and familial and community networks (sometimes involving white patrons and friends). However, the state of Virginia did attempt to limit opportunities for Black people to subvert the law by creating "Free Negro Registers" and limiting where these people could travel within the state. Individuals who remained in the state and were listed on the registers were then subject to vagrancy laws that limited their mobility in the Commonwealth. Free Black Virginians lived within a system that legally designed laws to keep them within the state and even more locally in the county if they did not leave upon manumission. Maintaining the number of free Blacks in the county was important, but the records show that it was a daunting task to keep the records straight when free Blacks purposely subverted the laws.[18]

Free Blacks did not always stay in the counties that manumitted them. There were only a few free Black people who were repeatedly listed for summons, in the registers, or even in the appeals to remain in the state following the Virginia state law that required free Blacks to register. The same could be said for Isle of Wight County and its smaller free Black population. The names that appear in records from Isle of Wight County within the same period likely do not cover all those free people who refused or neglected to answer their court summons.

The complex interplay between free Black individuals and local courts was repeated throughout Virginia and across the slave states more broadly. As a form of resistance, the ways in which free Black people navigated the court system and laws of the state demonstrate how they could identify and exploit weak points in a legal system that sought to repress them. Whether because of the value they brought to their communities through, for example, their place in the agricultural workforce, or simply because of white indifference to their presence, free Black people were able to resist pressure at both the state and local levels. This is an area that requires our attention if we wish to explain the various social dynamics of free Blacks during the antebellum period. Research on free Blacks and the various forms of resistance is growing to show that many free Blacks had the agency to maintain their liberties despite the laws of the state. In many counties, the laws of the state were not followed strictly. However, the evidence that we have shows the dynamics of social and economic changes taking place in Virginia during the antebellum period and the shifting roles of free Black people within their communities. To truly understand what it meant for some Black Virginians to be free within a slave society, we must strive to understand the world they lived in and their efforts to realize their independence on their own terms.

Chapter 4

Joseph Jenkins Roberts, Free Black Émigrés, and the Liberian Experiment

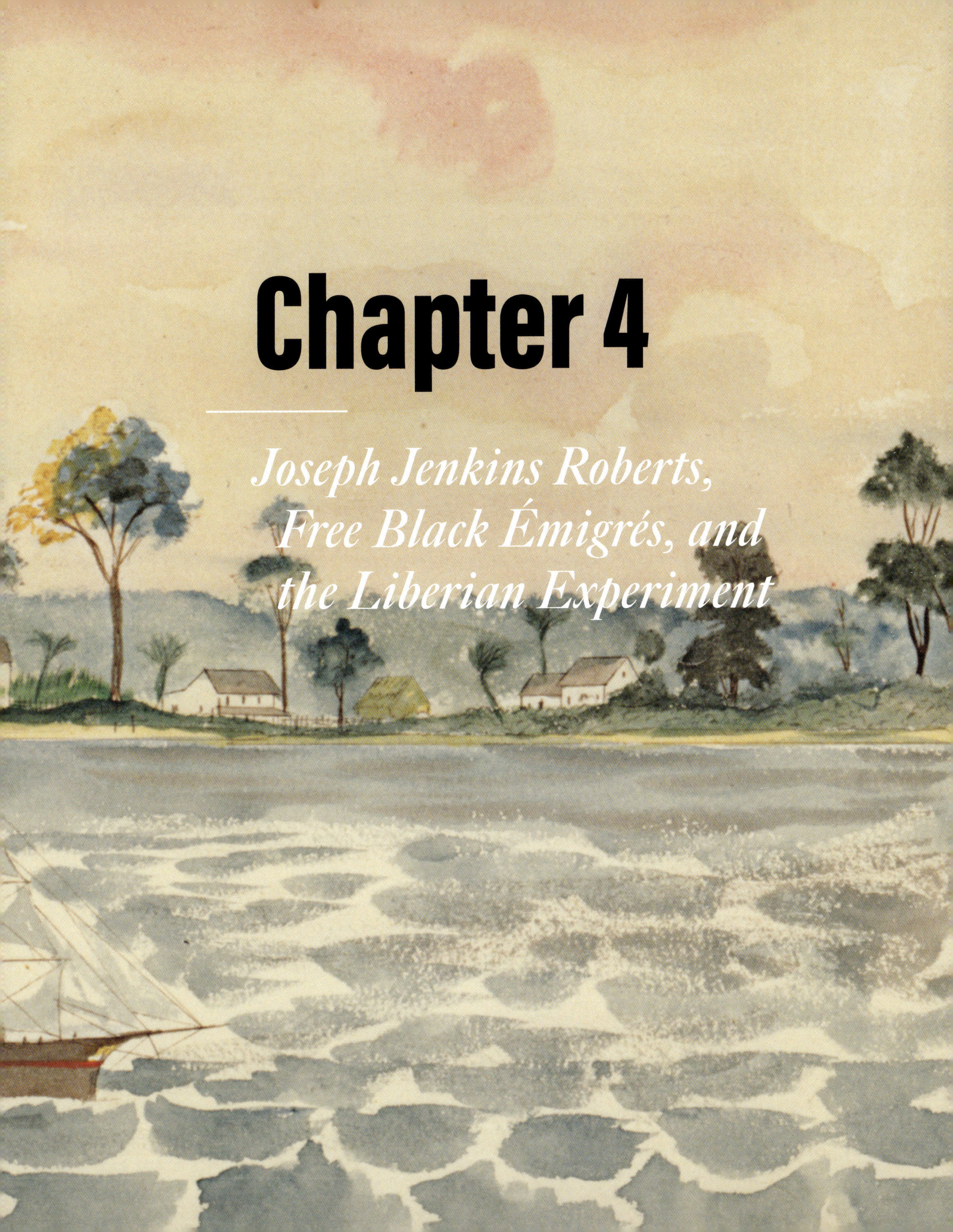

4

Joseph Jenkins Roberts, Free Black Émigrés, and the Liberian Experiment

Cassandra L. Newby-Alexander

When the Reverend Abraham Cheeseman left Norfolk in 1829, he was not alone. Accompanied by his wife and six children, he was destined for the colony of Liberia, where hundreds of others from the United States now resided. When they left, the Cheeseman family was part of a group of 127 émigrés who departed aboard the *Harriet* on an uncertain journey to a distant colony with only the promise of true liberty and freedom. Others had already left with the same hope. Forty-eight departed from Norfolk harbor four years before, in 1825, and even more a year later. Some of those intrepid émigrés included seven members of the Cooper family, Peggy Watts, Thomas Wilson, and John Jones. Others from different parts of Virginia joined them. From Richmond, there were couples (Lomax, Lewis, Dandridge, Spriggs). Numerous family groups (including three from the Brown family, three from the Elliott family, four from the Munroe family, five from the Parker family, sixteen from the Payne family, six from the Richardson family, and four from the Thomas family) and many individuals came from a broad swath of Virginia. Those areas included Albemarle County, Bedford County, Brunswick County, Fredericksburg, Lynchburg, Portsmouth, and Petersburg, just to name a few.

To understand the enormity of the departures between 1820 and 1865, sixty-four counties, thirty-eight cities, and 190 towns had émigrés traveling from Virginia to Liberia.[1]

This essay explores the story of the free Black émigrés from Virginia who created the nation of Liberia, highlighting a few, such as Liberia's first president, Joseph Jenkins Roberts, and how their accounts mirrored the complicated issues of race, colorism, belonging, and the quest for freedom that existed in the United States. Roberts and other émigrés carved autonomous spaces denied to them in the United States, because the colony of Liberia was established as a place to "repatriate" Black people to Africa. Yet, it also represented another space in the world in which outsiders colonized regions of a continent without invitation. Even though these colonizers were of African descent, many of them were culturally American and ethnically different from the people who lived in the region later called Liberia. This cultural divide would dominate Liberia's history and add to the clash of culture that ultimately led to a period of destabilization in the mid-twentieth century.

Initially, many free Black people in the United States railed against this effort by the American Colonization Society (ACS) to seemingly strengthen the institution of slavery by extracting free Black people from America. However, as white lawmakers constructed increasingly restrictive laws and policies that imperiled their freedoms, some free Black people—especially from southern states most impacted by these constraints, such as Virginia—began to regard the colony more as a refuge from white violence and discrimination than as a place of banishment.[2]

The large numbers of Virginia émigrés to Liberia reflected both the support that emancipation and colonization had among white and free Black people and the pressure exerted by public officials associated with the ACS on the free and enslaved population in the South. Despite the lack of support from free Black people in many northern states, free Black Virginians had a relatively positive attitude towards migration, which was tied more to the politics of the state, especially by the early nineteenth century. They believed that it was impossible to have full citizenship in Virginia because of the white population's fear of free Black people. The state's enslavers also used the promise of freedom for family groups as an enticement to emigrate.

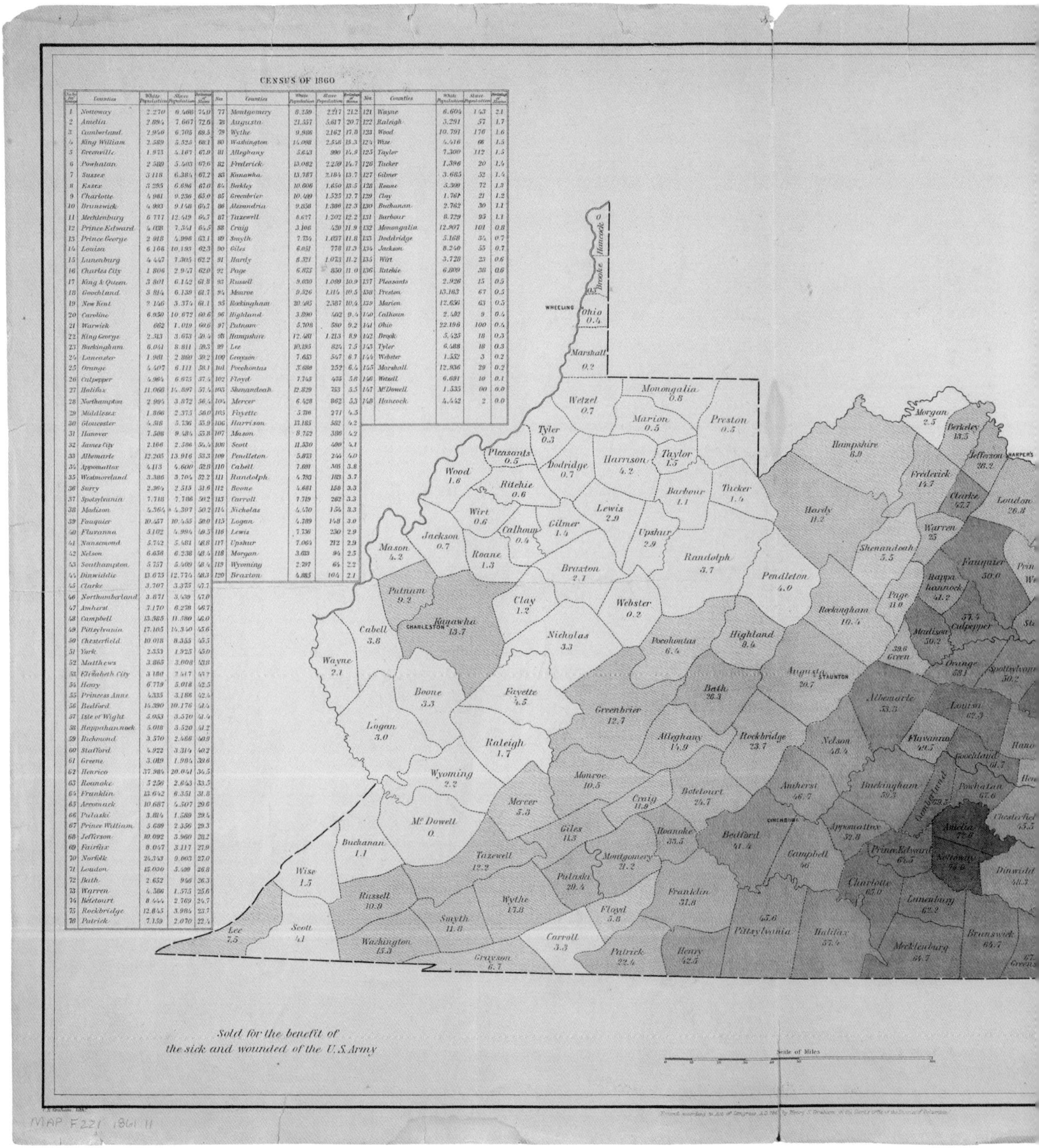

CENSUS OF 1860
WHEELING
Hancock
Brooke
Ohio 0.4
Marshall 0.2
Wetzel 0.7
Monongalia 0.8
Marion 0.5
Preston 0.5
Tyler 0.3
Pleasants 0.5
Doddridge 0.7
Harrison 4.2
Taylor 1.5
Wood 1.6
Ritchie 0.6
Barbour 1.1
Tucker 1.4
Wirt 0.6
Calhoun 0.4
Gilmer 1.4
Lewis 2.9
Upshur 2.9
Jackson 0.7
Roane 1.3
Mason 4.2
Braxton 2.1
Randolph 3.7
Putnam 9.2
Kanawha 13.7
CHARLESTON
Clay 1.2
Webster 0.2
Pendleton 4.0
Cabell 3.8
Nicholas 3.3
Pocahontas 6.4
Highland 8.4
Wayne 2.1
Boone 3.3
Fayette 4.5
Bath 26.3
Greenbrier 12.7
Logan 3.0
Raleigh 1.7
Alleghany 14.9
Rockbridge 23.7
Wyoming 2.2
Monroe 10.5
Mercer 5.3
Craig 11.9
Botetourt 24.7
Mc Dowell 0
Buchanan 1.1
Tazewell 12.2
Giles 11.3
Roanoke 35.5
Montgomery 21.2
Pulaski 29.4
Wise 1.5
Russell 10.9
Smyth 11.6
Wythe 17.8
Floyd 5.8
Franklin 31.8
Lee 7.5
Scott 4.1
Washington 15.3
Carroll 3.3
Grayson 6.7
Patrick 22.4
Henry 42.5
Pittsylvania
Halifax
Morgan 2.5
Berkeley 13.5
Jefferson 26.2
HARPER'S
Hampshire 6.9
Frederick 14.7
Clarke 47.7
Loudon 26.8
Hardy 11.2
Warren 25
Shenandoah 5.5
Fauquier 50.0
Rappahannock 41.2
Page 11.0
Rockingham 10.4
Madison 50.2
Culpepper
Green
Orange
Spottsylvania 50.2
Augusta 20.7
STAUNTON
Albemarle 53.3
Louisa 62.3
Nelson 48.4
Fluvanna 49.5
Goochland 61.7
Amherst 46.7
Buckingham 59.5
Powhatan 67.6
Cumberland
Bedford 41.4
Appomattox 52.8
Amelia 72.6
Chesterfield 45.5
Campbell 46
Prince Edward 64.5
Nottoway 74.6
Dinwiddie 48.3
Charlotte 67.0
Lunenburg 62.2
Mecklenburg 64.7
Brunswick 64.7
Sold for the benefit of the sick and wounded of the U.S. Army
Scale of Miles
MAP F221 1861 11

Virginia had the largest enslaved population in the nation and was home to a burgeoning domestic slave trade that transported thousands annually to the Lower South. It also had the largest free Black population in the nation until the 1840s, when Maryland eclipsed Virginia with approximately 10,000 more free people. Many free Black Virginians were convinced that emigration would free them from the increasing restrictions established by the state's leadership, especially before 1840. Furthermore, despite promises, the North held no special allure because of the socioeconomic struggles that were continually experienced by their free counterparts there. Many wrote letters explaining their desire to construct their identities as Americans and as people of African descent. They believed that only outside of the United States could their advocacy help to free their enslaved brothers and sisters. Unlike their northern counterparts, southern free Black people were convinced that they would never be able to gain full citizenship in the country because of racism and the prevalence of slavery. Moving northward would not change this dynamic. Instead, they wrote that their voices would be a more powerful inspiration to those in the United States if they ruled an all-Black nation.

Map Showing the Distribution of the Slave Population of the Southern States of the United States (detail), entered according to Act of Congress by Henry S. Graham, 1861. *Library of Congress*

Thus, almost one-third of all the émigrés to Liberia came from Virginia, while a full half came from the Chesapeake states of Virginia and Maryland.[3]

In 1670 and 1691, Virginia legislators passed laws prohibiting the free Black population from purchasing white Christians and mandating that they be transported out of the state if recently freed. It was the Great Awakening of religious fervor in the eighteenth century that opened opportunities and freedoms for supposedly free Black people. A retraction of rights reemerged in the post-Revolutionary years beginning in 1793 and accelerating following the unprecedented unrest among the enslaved population in all of Virginia's cities located along the waterways, culminating in Nat Turner's Rebellion of 1831. Restrictive laws specifically emerged between 1793 and 1831, in part because of the explosion of the free Black population that occurred primarily in Virginia, Maryland, and Delaware. These manumissions were driven by military service during the Revolutionary War and the War of 1812, successful efforts by freedom seekers, and the religious revival movement. As the numbers grew, so did white fears and stereotypes that depicted Black people as criminal and responsible for lowering the property values of homes. Thomas Jefferson's *Notes on the State of Virginia* added to these negative perceptions with his arguments that, as Black people were freed, they needed to be colonized to rid the nation of their dangerous presence which could also sully the "pure blood" of white people. Moreover, Jefferson wrote that Black people were incapable of competing with white people if they were freed, thus creating a drain on society.[4]

Jefferson's position highlights the numerous concerns around a large Black population at a time when the nation was struggling to establish its footprint internationally, even while shipping more of its agricultural products abroad. As planters and business leaders were busy restoring trade and plantation production, a new focus on cotton restructured the political, social, and economic landscape of the nation, ensuring the permanence of slavery and the increasing hostility toward free Black people in America. The country was also struggling to establish itself as an independent nation following the signing of the Peace of Paris in 1783.[5]

So fearful were Virginia lawmakers about the growing free Black population and the possibility that the insurrection which had occurred in Haiti would happen in their state that they made the decision to require all free Black Virginians to register their whereabouts with city or county clerks, carry

Burning of the Plaine du Cap, Haiti, French School, 1794, engraving. *© Archives Charmet / Bridgeman Images*

free papers to establish their status, and include detailed physical descriptions of themselves in the official records. Beginning in 1793, free Black people were caught up in an international threat to slaveholding primarily because of the Haitian Revolution that began when free Black people in Saint-Domingue (present-day Haiti) revolted against the white colonizers who were determined to restrict their rights just as France expanded the rights of all Black people and eliminated slavery. In July of that year, a fleet of 137 ships sailed into Norfolk harbor with 3,000 people from the former French colony of Saint-Domingue. This group included free and enslaved Black people and white people who brought stories about the horrors of the revolution and the fighting. There was also the belief that enslaved refugees contributed to the general unrest among Black people in the region. Moreover, hundreds of white and Black seamen and enslaved Black people intermingled on the busy streets of town, highlighting the commercial and mercantile prosperity of the area and foretelling the port city's importance in the wars in Europe and the opening of West Indian trade to the United States. Although the Haitian Revolution eventually expanded to the enslaved, white people believed that it was free Black people who destabilized slaveholding societies.[6]

Seven years after Haitian refugees reached Virginia, the Commonwealth was shaken when word got out about the slave Gabriel's rebellion conspiracy in 1800 and the belief that those from Saint-Domingue were involved. Conspirators were claimed to be everywhere from Richmond to Norfolk, leaving the white population determined that free Black people were a danger to the peace and security of the state. While this issue was debated, six years later legislators passed a law requiring that recently freed Black people had a year to leave the state or else become enslaved again. Free Black Virginians were also barred from testifying against white people in court and could be physically punished if a white person made a complaint against them even without any evidence to support their claims.[7]

At the same time that the Commonwealth was restricting the rights and liberties of free Black Virginians, the Great Awakening helped expand religion to its population. New denominations flourished, and Black people began to form their own congregations or join the recently formed Baptist and Methodist churches. It was within these denominations that the boundaries of race and gender loosened, albeit temporarily, with some white Baptists and Methodists even speaking out against slavery and supporting the expansion of rights for all Black people. The hope from religious evangelists was that these churches would begin changing the political landscape that supported slavery. What emerged in the wake of the religious revivalism of the late eighteenth century was a more active and involved free Black presence in the religious life of the Commonwealth. While enslaved and free Black people were heavily involved in worshipping in "hush harbors" in rural areas and in Baptist, Catholic, and Methodist churches in urban communities, free Black people helped to establish Black-dominated churches. For example, in Norfolk, free Black people helped establish the first Methodist Episcopal Church (later known as Zion Methodist and then United Methodist Church) on Cumberland Street in 1793. So supportive was the free Black community that the church had 692 members seven years later. In the 1790s, Portsmouth's Court Street Baptist

Church hired an enslaved man, Jacob Bishop, who was a licensed minister, to preach in the church, attracting large numbers of Black and white members. Black churches continued to grow in every city and town in Virginia, such that by the 1830s, the Zion Baptist Church, First Baptist Church of Williamsburg, Colored Methodist churches in Norfolk and Portsmouth, First Baptist Church in Norfolk, First Baptist Church of Petersburg, and First African Baptist Church of Richmond had all been formed.[8]

In 1812, the wealthiest Black person in the United States owned a fleet of trading vessels anchored in Tagrin Bay in the British colony of Sierra Leone.

First African Baptist Church, 1865, photograph. *Library of Congress*

A year earlier, Paul Cuffee, a free Black New England Quaker, shipmaster, and whaling merchant, had established the cooperative organization "Friendly Society of Sierra Leone," with the goal of facilitating good relations between émigrés and the local populations. When he arrived in the town near Tagrin Bay, walking around the locality gave him an idea of how Black Americans could create their own society, far removed from the racism in the United States. When he ran into problems with U.S. Customs because of trade disagreements with Britain, his appeal allowed him to have a meeting with President James Madison and the Treasury Secretary Albert Gallatin. During that meeting, Cuffee suggested the repatriation to Africa of freed and free Black people. By forming their own colony in West Africa, Black people could lead their own nation while evangelizing the local populations. His idea gained interest from Madison who believed, like Jefferson, that the enmity that existed between Black and white people would not go away.[9]

Silhouette of Captain Paul Cuffee, from a drawing by John Pole, 1812, engraving. *Library of Congress*

Although Paul Cuffee would die before realizing his plans, James Madison, Chief Justice John Marshall, and others would be intricately involved in organizing the American Colonization Society in 1816. Following in the footsteps of Britain, with its colony of Sierra Leone, the ACS sought to establish a colony in West Africa to promote the repatriation of Black people to the continent. Founded by Presbyterian minister Robert Finley and a coalition of white politicians and ministers from the North and the South, the ACS was led by Supreme Court Justice Bushrod Washington, Speaker of the House Henry Clay, future President Andrew Jackson, Treasury Secretary William Crawford, Congressman and later Senator Daniel Webster, District Attorney Francis Scott Key, and Virginia congressman John Randolph. These men composed the upper echelons of the U.S. government and framed its political national outlook. From the

Bushrod Washington, Chester Harding, 1828, oil on canvas. *National Portrait Gallery, Smithsonian Institution; gift of the Washington family, with thanks to the many Washingtons who valued this painting and preserved it for nearly two centuries*

beginning, it appeared the primary focus of the ACS was to remove free Black people from the country because their growing presence was perceived as a source of friction with slaveholding America. Free Black people represented "freedom and self-reliance," though members of the ACS also deemed them as unassimilable. Other ACS supporters rationalized their support, claiming this was an opportunity for free Black people to occupy leadership positions on a continent they believed did not consider them "alien."[10]

Finley's suggestion of having free Black people serve as missionaries to the newly formed colony of Liberia promoted the idea of expanding a religious message to Africa with the support of the American Colonization Society. However, Paul Cuffee warned Finley that, while creating a colony could facilitate a place of empowerment for Black people, Black leaders must be consulted before publicizing any plans for African colonization. On first look, northern Black leadership, which included James Forten, Richard Allen, and Daniel Coker, did provide support. However, once the ACS's plans were presented to the larger community, the pushback was overwhelming. President James Monroe accepted their overall objective—as did every U.S. president afterward, including Abraham Lincoln—and he approved government funding. Moreover, the Monroe administration accepted the ACS's agent as its representative in West Africa and had Congress appropriate $100,000 as the first of a series of grants that would purchase land, construct forts and homes, pay teachers and colonial administrators, and acquire farming equipment for the settlers.[11]

Determined to persuade Black people to emigrate, the ACS had agents stationed in every city in Virginia. One of those agents was the Reverend William H. Starr, pastor of the Colored Methodist Church in Norfolk. During the lag in convincing the African American community to leave during the 1840s and 1850s, he wrote to the ACS expressing his frustration, especially with the members of his church and the larger community. Zealously preaching colonization, Starr believed he had harangued individuals enough to follow his advice and leave the country. Despite his efforts, however, he had to write a disappointing letter to the ACS office, stating, "I regret to tell you that my 15 or 20 got down to 12 a week ago, and from information received from them today, it is doubtful now whether more than four will be ready." In 1853, Starr confessed in another letter to the ACS that of the "250 which I counted on, there will hardly be more than fifty." Somehow, he believed his lack of success in convincing free Black Americans to leave the country, even when they initially agreed, was because of the untruthfulness of Black people rather than his pressure tactics. What Starr refused to understand was that free Blacks claimed the United States as their home, and most were unwilling to leave.[12]

On March 3, 1819, when Congress authorized the return to Africa of captured people found on board ships that were engaged in the now-illegal slave trade, President Monroe took advantage of the law to support colonization. Anxious to authorize the state-funded removal of free Black people from the United States, Monroe extended the interpretation of this law to include the establishment of an American colony in West Africa as the vehicle for repatriation in a special message to Congress on December 19, 1819. This allowed for the first intrepid group of eighty-eight people (thirty-three men, eighteen women, and thirty-seven children) to settle in Liberia via the 300-ton brig *Elizabeth* in cooperation with the ACS. The three-masted *Elizabeth* left New York City's North River during an extremely cold February in 1820. Two-thirds of the primarily literate men, women, and children came from New York and Pennsylvania, and they were

Plan of the U.S.S. *Alligator*, C. Ware, about 1840. *Courtesy of the Naval History and Heritage Command*

Longitude East from Washington.
REMARKS.
The Colony of Liberia extends from Gallinas river to the Territory of Kroo Settra, a distance of about 280 miles in length, along the Coast,* & from 20 to 30 miles inland, (in some places much more;) it includes within its Jurisdiction, the territories of several native tribes, the names of which are as follows: the Feys or Veys occupy the country from Gallinas R. to Little Cape Mount, a distance of about 50 miles along the coast, and 25 to 30 miles inland: they are an active warlike and proud people. Population 12,000 to 15,000. The Dey Tribe extends from Little Cape Mount to Mesurado river about 30 miles in length, and 12 to 16 miles inland: an indolent & inoffensive people. Pop. 6000 to 8,000
The Bassa Tribes extend from Mesurado River, southward: they are generally domestic, industrious and averse to war, and supposed to be in numbers about 125,000 souls. The country abounds in rice, oil and cattle, and rivals in fertility any part of the African coast.
At a distance of from 30 to 50 miles inland, a belt of dense and almost impassable forest occurs along the whole of this coast, of from one to two days journey in breadth, which nearly prevents all intercourse between the maritime and interior tribes, and is one of the principal causes why the inland parts of this section of Africa are so entirely unknown to the civilised world.
* The territory at present under the actual jurisdiction of the Colony, extends from Grand Cape Mount, to Trade Town, a distance of about 150 miles.
The Pissou River has been traced 100 miles from the sea, and affords a safe navigation of 1½ days sail.
The St. Pauls River is supposed to have a course of from 250 to 300 miles.
Country of the Kittims
Country of the Feys or Veys
Country of the Deys
Country of the Grain
Monrovia
Cape Mesurado
Millsburg
Caldwell
Stockton
Junk River District
Junk Territory
Little Bassa
Grand Bassa
Grand Colo
Trade Town
Grand Cape Mount
C. Mount Landing. Mountain fronting to 1000 ft. above the sea
Free Town
Colony of Sierra Leone
Bootams
Timanees
ATLANTIC OCEAN
WINDWARD COAST
MAP of the WEST COAST OF AFRICA, from SIERRA LEONE to CAPE PALMAS; including the Colony of LIBERIA: Compiled chiefly from the SURVEYS and OBSERVATIONS of the LATE REVd. J. ASHMUN.
Scale of Miles.
5 10 20 30 40 50 60 70 80 90 100
Published by A. Finley Philada.
1830
J.H. Young Sc.
Longitude West from Greenwich.

listed as black or mulatto with skills that ranged from tradesmen to farmers.[13]

The British government refused to allow the settlers to disembark at Freetown, Sierra Leone. They were forced instead to go to Sherbro Island, the site of an old British fort, some 75 miles distant. A year later, the *Augusta* arrived in Sierra Leone to retrieve those surviving settlers and continued on to Cape Mesurado, accompanied by the U.S.S. *Alligator*. Thus, after this false start on Sherbro Island off the coast of Sierra Leone, Lieutenant Robert Stockton of the U.S. Navy led an expedition to Cape Mesurado in Liberia in December 1821. The *Alligator* was one of five schooners built for the suppression of slavery and piracy during Monroe's presidency. Interestingly, it was Lieutenant Matthew Perry, later to gain fame as the Commodore of the African Squadron and leading figure in the opening of Japan to Western influence, who mapped the landing site of Cape Mesurado, the location of present-day Monrovia.[14]

When Stockton arrived, he led a protracted and heated discussion reportedly at the point of a gun, with Kings Peter, Jimmy, Governor, Zoda, George, and Long Peter of the Grand Bassa, Bassa, and chieftains of the Dei, to agree to the deed of a sixty-mile strip of land to the American

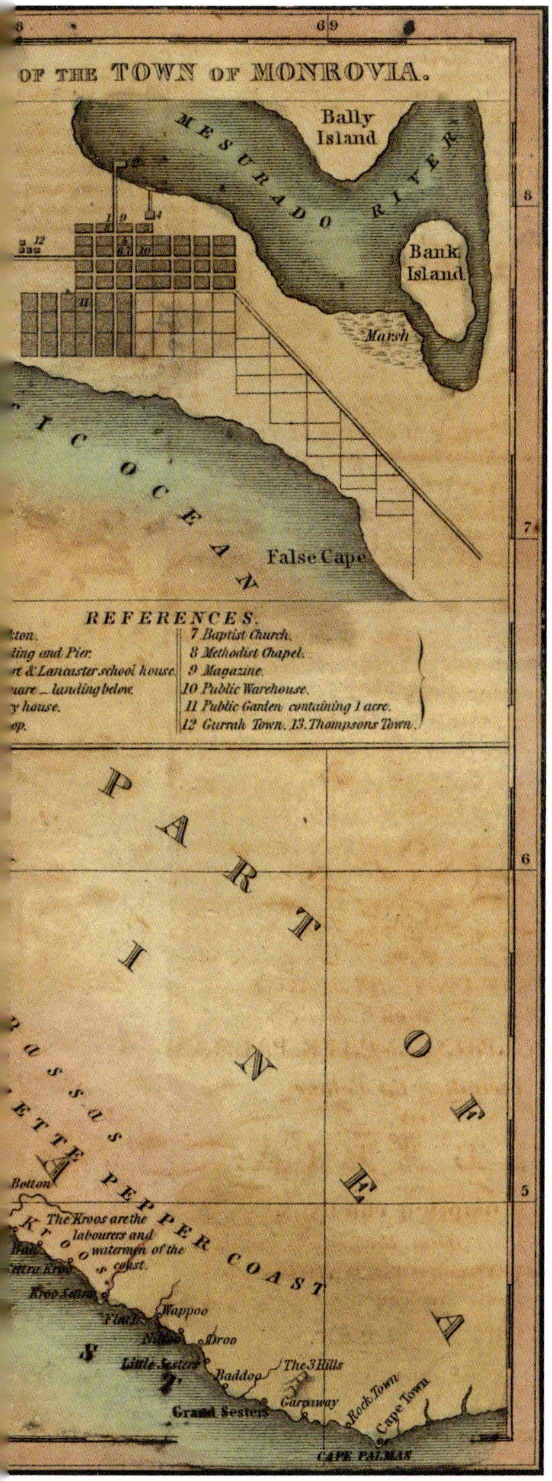

Cape Mesurado appears in the center of the coastline in this *Map of the West Coast of Africa from Sierra Leone to Cape Palmas, including the Colony of Liberia*, J. Ashmun, J. H. Young, and A. Finley (Philadelphia, Pa.: A. Finley, 1830). *Library of Congress*

Colonization Society, from Cape Mesurado to the Junk River, in exchange for goods and supplies (which included weapons) valued at $300. An agreement (referred to as the Duker Contract) was also secured, whereby the locals would allow the settlers to live in peace, provided they did not disturb the Bassa trade network, which included the slave trade.[15]

The land paid for by the United States and ACS representatives became the site of the capital of Liberia, Monrovia. Although it appears that a land survey was not conducted, an 1824 map illustrated the approximately 140 acres of land that was involved in the transaction. The document that confirms this sale was signed by ACS agent Eli Ayres and U.S. Navy Lieutenant Robert Stockton, commander of the U.S.S. *Alligator*, as the buyers. The vendors were the six Bassa kings—Peter, George, Zoda, Long Peter, Governor, and Jimmy—who were the local leaders.[16]

Although the ACS acquired the property under this charter or agreement, the organization did not exercise governing authority. Of course, these "land deeds" were devised from a Western perspective and negotiated with a culture that had no concept of individual ownership; rather, land was communally held, with the chief speaking for the collective body. By the late 1820s, however, the Bassa chiefs had second thoughts about the sale, especially after the ACS leader, Jehudi Ashmun, attempted to stop the vigorous slave trading. The Bassa—egged on by European slave traders, particularly the Spanish and French—saw this as "tantamount to a declaration of war." The fledgling colony was faced with possible annihilation, but the U.S. Navy offered support. Once opposition was minimized and slave trading was greatly reduced, the colony was on surer footing, even though it still struggled.[17]

In 1827, the Maryland Colonization Society established an independent colony at Cape Palmas, while Virginians settled at Marshall under ACS jurisdiction. In 1835, the Young Men's Colonization Society of Pennsylvania also founded a settlement at the mouth of the St. John River, with its own governor and with the cooperation of the New York Colonization Society. Three years later, the Mississippi Colonization Society established a settlement at the mouth of the Sinoe River. Shortly after the Mississippi Society set up shop, the ACS authorized the Commonwealth of Liberia to orchestrate the merger of these various settlements, led by Thomas Buchanan, brother of future U.S. President James Buchanan. Buchanan had been the governor of Bassa Cove and was appointed by the ACS as governor of Liberia. By contrast, the lieutenant governor was elected by the settlers, as was the Council, the legislative body. Yet, the ACS maintained tight control over Liberian operations because it could veto any legislation the Council enacted.[18]

Rev. Lott Cary (1780–1828), from *History of the Negro Church*, by Carter G. Woodson (Washington, D.C.: The Associated Publishers, 1921). *VMHC*

For the white patrons and supporters of the Liberian colony who wanted to present a friendlier face to colonization, this landscape was seen as a space for Christian missions and a site where Western culture could be transplanted onto African soil by those of African descent. But many did not believe that Black people were capable of self-governance; they simply wanted them extracted from the United States. For Black Americans, however, Liberia represented much more than an escape from white hate. It allowed them to claim a place in African society that, for many, was distant from their memory and DNA. Those Black émigrés were determined to demonstrate how they could govern a nation and create a powerful base for Black people around the world. This goal was especially important as the world witnessed the rise of white supremacist arguments that labeled Black people as inherently inferior or animal-like. The irony of Liberia, however, was that the very people who had such lofty aspirations would, in turn, deny the indigenous populations their rights, similar to what occurred in the United States.[19]

The Roberts family in Virginia may have heard about the hardships experienced by Lott Cary and the first group of émigrés who arrived in Liberia. These hardships included limited supplies, the challenges of clearing lots and building homes, and a hostile population who did not welcome the intrusion of the interlopers. Moreover, the ACS's support was not substantial. Nonetheless, some émigrés were satisfied with their conditions, although they experienced homesickness.[20]

Twenty years before Joseph Jenkins Roberts was born, Black people made up 45 percent of the total population in Norfolk. Forty-three percent were enslaved, and two percent were free. Statewide, the numbers were even more significant, with 2,000 in 1782 and 20,000 by 1800. By 1810, the free Black population had increased tenfold in Norfolk, generated primarily through natural reproduction, manumissions, family- and self-purchase, and migration from other areas, such as North Carolina. Not surprisingly, these increases generated fear statewide from the white slaveholding leadership, especially in such cities as Norfolk because of its port that brought people from around the world. And in this urban environment, Black people moved about with relative freedom, and enslaved people often lived apart from their owners in Black communities. The white leadership in Virginia grew increasingly fearful of these communities and of the potential threat they posed to slaveholding society if they organized.[21]

American Colonization Society token, 1833, copper. *VMHC*

So it was that the evangelical spirit of manumission that began in the eighteenth century bore fruit in the early nineteenth century, with growing classes of free people of color who occupied a more privileged position in society though still without access to power or political influence. James and Amelia Roberts, a middle-class couple who lived in Norfolk, offered such an example. James was a free Black boatman and successful businessman who carried goods and engaged in commerce between Petersburg and Norfolk, while his mother took care of the children born to the couple. One of those children was Joseph Jenkins Roberts, future president of Liberia, born on March 15, 1809, during this transformative period in Virginia's history, when free Black people, who were often part of the wealthy class of people of mixed ancestry, saw their rights dwindle with each passing year. Many of Norfolk's city leaders joined the American Colonization Society, forming one of the earliest chapters in the city because of the large free Black community. Working-class white people were also in support of the ACS because it was a way to rid the city of Black economic competitors. Perhaps more than in other locations, all the prominent ACS members were slaveholders, and this sent the wrong message to free Black people because they perceived the ACS as merely a scheme to remove them from the country, even though the United States was their home. It may have been pressure from the Norfolk ACS agent that led James Roberts to make the decision to move his family to Petersburg and spend several years expanding their trade business into new locations, including Liberia.[22]

The Roberts family left their home in Petersburg and traveled to Norfolk where they boarded the *Harriet* bound for Liberia in March 1829, along with 155 passengers who included more than one hundred free Black people from Petersburg and Richmond. A few other families, such as the Jacob Snyder family, arrived from Harpers Ferry via Baltimore. Many left the country in search of freedom and a desire to spread the Gospel, while others like the Roberts family emigrated because of a desire to expand their trade business. This was the first time a large and self-organized transit was arranged, and Norfolk was the primary departure point in Virginia. Émigrés arrived by train, cart, or ship. Once they were in the city, ACS agent John McPhail arranged to temporarily house them in free Black and white ACS members' homes until their ship left. McPhail's other duty was to ensure that no one changed their mind about leaving. Apparently, some free Black people in Norfolk were suspicious of the ACS's motivations and shared their sentiments freely. Because of the fear that enslaved people bound for Liberia would take the opportunity to disappear, the ACS orchestrated a sentimental and public departure ceremony filled with speakers, prayers, and hymns. A few times, slaveholders of formerly enslaved people spoke kindly of the person, asking them to stay in touch.[23]

The Roberts family were not the only ones involved in the trade business. Because the goal was to become self-sufficient, Lott Cary and Colston Waring, a missionary for the African Baptist Missionary Society of Petersburg, had organized the Mesurado Channeling Company, a joint stock company. This company traded in goods ranging from agricultural products and alcohol to firearms and other munitions. The Roberts family were part of the trading firm of Roberts, Colson, and Company. This was one of many firms owned by prominent free Black people in the country. So prosperous were these companies that collectively they were considered part of the Monrovian

Joseph Jenkins Roberts (1809–1876), Rufus Anson, 1854, daguerreotype. *Library of Congress*

Jane Roberts (d. 1911), Rufus Anson, 1854, daguerreotype. *Library of Congress*

merchant elite, a close-knit community of business leaders who intermarried and intersected politically, economically, and socially.[24]

So it was that after 1829, thousands came from twenty-seven states across the nation, but especially from the Upper South. Most emigrated to Liberia between 1820 and 1865 on "their own volition." About 4,500 were free Black people; 1,000 were freed by their owners, with no stipulation that emigration to Liberia was a requirement for manumission; and 6,000 were emancipated by their owners on the condition they emigrate. Virginia's African American immigrants made up the largest group of émigrés, followed by residents of North Carolina, Georgia, Tennessee, South Carolina, Kentucky, Maryland, and Mississippi.[25]

Except for Haiti, Liberia has the distinction of being the oldest of the world's Black republics. Located a few degrees north of the equator, in the southwest corner of the western bulge of Africa, the nation is 43,000 square miles, extending 370 miles along the Atlantic coast between Sierra Leone and Ivory Coast. About the size of Tennessee, the nation has a similar heritage to its neighbor, Sierra Leone. Colonized by those from the African Diaspora in the United States, the nation has its cultural footprints squarely in the American political, social, and economic sphere.[26]

When the African American émigrés arrived, they were surrounded by anywhere from sixteen to twenty distinct ethnic groups, including the Kpelle, Kissi, Gola, Grebo, Kru, Mandingo, Bassa, Belle, Dey Gbandi, Gio, Krahn, Loma, Mano, Mende, and Vai. These groups spoke at least twenty different languages and dialects, and they practiced their native religions and Islam. The Bassa, Kru, and Grebo lived along the coast and were the largest of all the ethnicities; even though the Mandingo and Fanti were present, they were relatively recent arrivals from the northeast and the Gold Coast, and they were regarded as foreigners. Ironically, even though the new African American arrivals regarded the continent as the "Promised Land," they were disinterested in integrating into African society. Instead, they believed they were still Americans and culturally

Map of Liberia, Randolph Coyle under the direction of William McLain (Baltimore, Md.: E. Weber & Co., 1845). *Library of Congress*

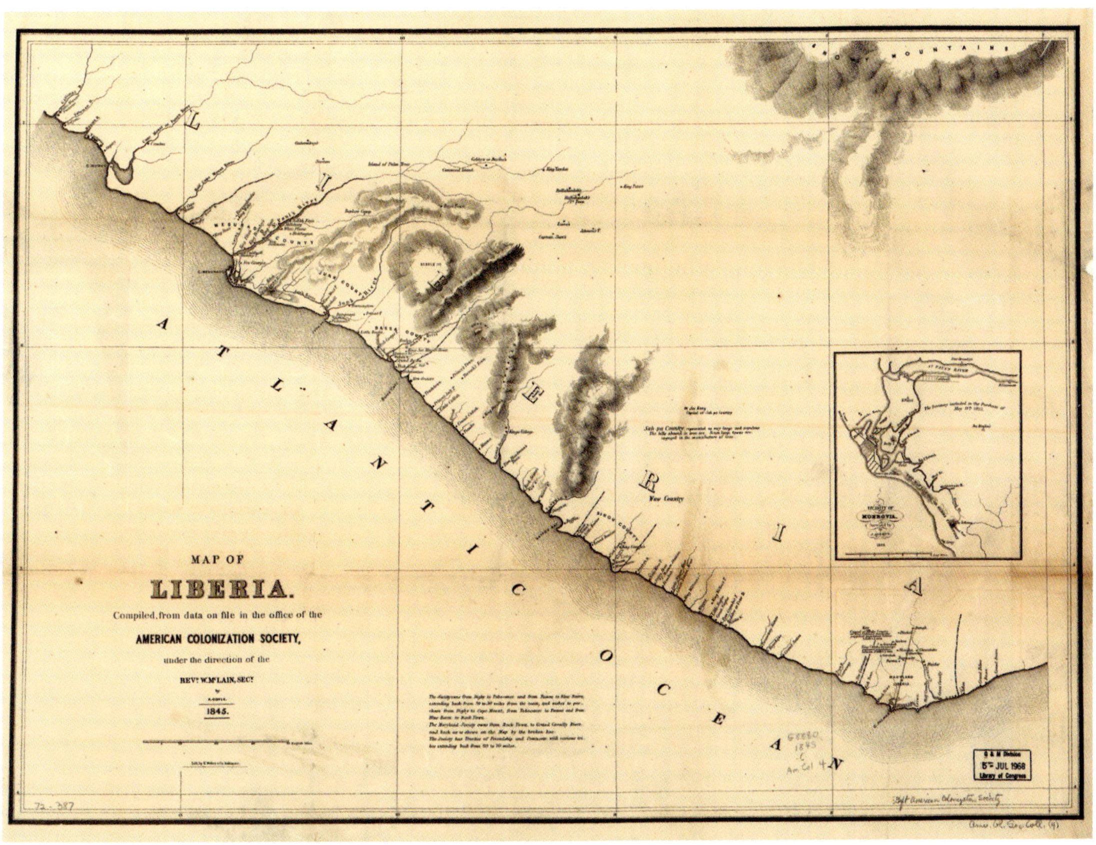

"Fish Town at Bassau, Liberia," Robert K. Griffith, 1856, watercolor. *Library of Congress*

superior to the Africans. The result was that they continued to uphold their social and cultural standards that came primarily from the American South.[27]

Once this immigrant group settled—primarily along the coastal area—they became known as Americo-Liberians. Never exceeding more than 5 percent of the nation's population, they nonetheless established a society modeled after the United States. And like their European-American counterparts, they restricted the indigenous populations to their own regions, with exceptions made when cheap labor requirements emerged. In fact, the Americo-Liberians established a planter aristocracy, sometimes forcibly recruiting laborers and engaging in compulsory labor practices. To their eventual detriment, this elite minority would exclude the indigenous majority from the nation's political and economic power for 133 years.[28]

The Americo-Liberians also established a hybrid version of the paramount chiefs' system to simplify the administration of government. Before this, the tribal organization revolved around clan rule in each town. When clan rule was brought under the control of the Liberian government, the people were regarded as part of the hinterlands and were administered by District Commissioners. Complicating this arrangement was the exclusion of native Africans as citizens of the colony, and the conflation of several groups and clans into the same district.[29]

Not surprisingly, those who emigrated found themselves regarded as aliens who threatened the indigenous populations. The Americo-Liberians were frequently called white men by the West Africans whom they encountered, partly because many of them were of mixed ancestry and also because they were culturally different. Many settlers seldom ventured far from the coastal towns and river settlements, unless leading a militia force. Those who came as missionaries were the exception because they moved to be near the groups they hoped to convert to Christianity. The Americo-Liberians also found themselves the unwanted stepchild of the United States, which steadfastly resisted recognizing Liberia as an official American colony, resulting in a myriad of complications for the Americo-Liberians, the ACS, and the U.S. government.[30]

When Joseph Jenkins Roberts arrived in Liberia in 1829, he entered politics, eventually becoming the high sheriff in 1833, whose chief duty was to collect taxes. He took part in the continuing militia forays into territory held by groups in active opposition to the American settlement. Although the ACS had envisioned a nation of farmers and missionaries, trade was clearly the only

Mansion-house of President Roberts, Monrovia, Liberia (A. Hoen & Co., about 1850). *Library of Congress*

source of money in Liberia, as in other colonial settlements. Roberts's company was more than prepared for this. Early on, he formed a trading partnership with William Colson, a Black Petersburg barber. Colson would ship basic supplies to Liberia, while Roberts would ship ivory, camwood, palm products, and other trade goods from the Liberian interior to their trade partners in Philadelphia. Yet, the ambitious young Roberts suffered tragedy, as did many in the first few decades in Liberia. In his first year in Monrovia, Roberts lost his first wife and infant child. He would later marry Jane Rose Waring, the daughter of Colston Waring, who arrived ten years after the first settlers.[31]

When a new constitution was written in 1838, Roberts was appointed lieutenant governor. After the death of the ACS-appointed white governor in 1840, Roberts became the first Black governor of Liberia. He held this post from 1842 to 1847. It was in 1844, during his period as governor, that he first returned to the United States and, over the next twenty-five years, he traveled frequently to the United States and England in efforts to raise funds for Liberia, obtain diplomatic recognition, and encourage emigration. Roberts also worked to strengthen Liberia by consolidating its land holdings through purchases, while simultaneously claiming sovereignty over lands that bordered Sierra Leone. He did this, in part, to end the slave trade in the region.[32]

Roberts recognized the confusion that Britain and France had about Liberia's sovereignty because of its relationship with the ACS, which was why he worked to officially sever that relationship. He was careful to note the obligation and deep gratitude that Liberia felt toward the ACS, theorizing that it would therefore not obstruct their efforts toward independence. The citizens of Liberia voted to determine if they wanted to declare independence. On October 27, 1846, and with two-thirds of the voters participating, a slight majority approved the call for independence. Though Roberts and the Council were disappointed that the vote was not overwhelmingly in favor of independence, they moved forward nonetheless. Roberts ended the discussion on the matter by introducing a resolution which would insist that the people's wishes were adhered to during the January 1847 Council session.[33]

Simon Greenleaf, Harvard Law School professor and president of the Massachusetts Colonization Society, crafted the nation's new constitution. Controversy quickly emerged, with the ACS requesting that the Constitution allow them to retain title to the land—a position many in the Council bitterly opposed.

What is most significant is that the Liberian "Declaration of Independence" did not actually declare political independence like the U.S. one did because, according to Roberts, from its inception Liberia was a free and sovereign state. Instead, the Declaration was a political manifesto that sought international recognition only.[34]

When the "Declaration of Independence" was issued in 1847, which officially severed ties with the ACS and established Liberia as a sovereign nation, the effect was to push the British colonies back. Those who settled near Cape Palmas from the Maryland Colonization Society, an offshoot of the ACS in 1831, continued as a separate and sovereign state until 1857, when this was annexed by Liberia under the Roberts presidency. Ironically, it was not until 1862, during Abraham Lincoln's administration, that the United States recognized Liberia's sovereignty, in stark contrast to Britain, presumably because the principal objectors were embroiled in rebellion against the federal government.[35]

The Roberts Administration, like those before it, was notable for its executive actions. Serving as president from January 1848 to 1856, and again from 1872 to 1876, Roberts focused on consolidating the nation's coastal areas and solidifying its boundaries, especially those under dispute with Sierra Leone. Roberts purchased land from local tribes, extending Liberia's boundary one hundred miles westward from Cape Mount to the Sewa River near Sherbro Island.[36]

Virginia émigré William Burke wrote letters that expressed enthusiasm about his experiences in Liberia, while also warning potential émigrés that they could expect hardships, like any first settlements in a new country. Echoing those sentiments during a return trip to Petersburg to publicize Liberia's accomplishments, Joseph Jenkins Roberts explained to a majority-white audience that Liberia was like Jamestown, filled with challenges that the colonists were overcoming to create a great nation.[37]

Throughout the nineteenth century, the American Colonization Society was responsible for transporting approximately 16,000 emigrants to Liberia in a reversal of the African Diaspora. Forty-one ships carried these mostly free Black men, women, and children from the United States to Liberia. Those who left the country's shores hoped for a new life, using migration as an agency for opportunity. Though they sought prosperity and freedom in a land occupied by multiple different ethnic groups, the behavior of many of these migrants would model that of America's twentieth-century European immigrants, leaving them distinct, separate, and eventually a target.

Chapter 5

Education, Politics, and the Legacy of Free Black Virginians after Emancipation

5

Education, Politics, and the Legacy of Free Black Virginians after Emancipation

Stephen Rockenbach

James Major Colson, Jr., a native of Petersburg, Virginia, and a recent graduate of Dartmouth College in New Hampshire, wrote a letter on April 21, 1883, to Alfred W. Harris inquiring about a position at a newly established school. Colson was asking about employment at the newly funded state institution for the education of Black Virginians to be staffed and led by Black educators. Harris was a lawyer, state delegate, and founder of the recently created Virginia Normal and Collegiate Institute (V.N.C.I.). Colson indicated that he was writing Harris "since you seem to be the leading spirit in this enterprise." Indeed, Harris introduced the bill proposing the creation of a place of higher education where "our Blacks, girls and boys, may go and drink from the fountain of knowledge until their ambition is satiated, and then step into the world prepared as good and upright citizens to meet its responsibilities." Harris had dedicated himself to supporting the uplift of other Black Virginians, using his influence and political connections to bring about the creation of this institute, which continues to

Members of the Virginia General Assembly, 1887–88, including Alfred W. Harris (1853–1920) (front row, left), from Luther P. Jackson, *Negro Office-Holders in Virginia, 1865–1895* (Norfolk, Va.: Guide Quality Press, 1945). *VMHC*

this day as Virginia State University. He was born free in 1854, to a family which had lived as free people in Fairfax and Prince William counties since the late eighteenth century. A graduate of Howard University Law School, Harris had an office in Petersburg and belonged to the Readjuster Party, which advocated "readjusting" the state's prewar debt and using tax money instead to fund education, health care, and infrastructure for both white and Black Virginians. With slavery now in the past, Harris, Colson, and other like-minded Black Virginians looked to the future, and the uplift of their communities.[1]

Harris and Colson had much in common. Both were educated men who belonged to prominent free Black families. Colson, no doubt, had heard of the plans for the Virginia Normal and Collegiate Institute from his family, who could trace their lineage back to James Colson, a free Black man who purchased land in Petersburg in 1804. Colson was eager to join the faculty of the new college and believed his family's reputation would aid him. In a second letter addressed to Major Branch on May 6, Colson explained that he was "taking it for granted that you know of me and that you have a fair idea of what grade of work my training at Dartmouth has fitted me for." Colson's efforts resulted in a position on the faculty of the V.N.C.I., teaching science for twenty-one years. Black Virginians highly valued education after emancipation, and individuals like Harris and Colson were positioned to help champion this cause because of their background and their own access to education, which would have been very rare among those who were previously enslaved.[2]

The transition from slavery to freedom that many Black Virginians experienced did not apply to those individuals who were previously free. Although recently emancipated freed people often had to navigate freedom with few resources, some free Black Americans had property and/or local status that allowed them to adjust to the dynamics of a post-slavery environment. Free Black people before 1865 had limitations on the extent of their freedom, which varied significantly by region, locality, time period, and a number of other variables. Still, their experience stood in stark contrast to enslaved Virginians, with the main distinction being control over their own labor and the ability to advocate for and protect family members. Because of this, the most distinct change brought about by emancipation for previously free Black families would be the potential for expanded legal rights, political participation, and stronger connections with formerly enslaved family, friends, and neighbors. Though Black residents before 1865 could own property and were liable for paying taxes, state law denied them important aspects of citizenship including voting, education, and holding political office. This meant that those who were free before the Civil War occupied a distinctly different position compared to those who were enslaved, and had different experiences, expectations, and obstacles, while still facing racism and discrimination. Thus, free Black Virginians had greater opportunities for community leadership, as in the case of James Major Colson, Jr. However, free status before the war was not necessarily a guarantee of success, nor was previous enslavement a harbinger of poverty. Instead, both free and formerly enslaved Virginians adjusted to a new system of white supremacy, one that categorized all Black Virginians together and fostered a system to restrict the rights and citizenship of them all in the same manner.

During enslavement, a caste system existed among Black southerners with free people located at the top of the hierarchy, but emancipation changed the dynamics and led to a new status quo. Before emancipation, free Black families, such as the Colson family in Petersburg, held a place in society based on their ability to own property, economic ties, and ability to aid people in their community, both free and enslaved. These connections between free and enslaved Black people were important, and included intermarriage, business relationships, family connections, and social interactions. But ties to white residents, both financial and biological, at times held an advantage for some free Blacks, though they served to further differentiate free people from those who were enslaved. For example, James Major Colson, Jr.'s mother, Fannie Meade Bolling, was mixed-race and bore the last name of the Bolling family, an influential white Virginia family. She herself worked for a white family in Petersburg as a house servant before marrying James Major Colson, Sr., in 1852, but she was given secret instruction in reading and writing. Fannie Meade Bolling's literacy was unusual; it was illegal for anyone to instruct Black Virginians in groups or for pay. Now Fannie Meade Colson, she was able to open a school for the newly emancipated in 1865, and she encouraged her nine children to pursue education. Her son, James Major Colson, Jr., was born in 1855, and attended a private school in Petersburg run by former Confederate officer, Giles B. Cook. Cook urged the young man to attend high school in Middleboro, Massachusetts, in 1877, which led to his admission to Dartmouth College and completion of his degree in 1883. Colson's letter to Alfred Harris demonstrates the young educator's dedication to service to others and the influence of his mother. James Major Colson, Jr.'s level of education would have been rare among Black Virginians, and while he gained his credentials in the North, he desired to return to Petersburg to be a part of the Virginia Normal and Collegiate Institute and Harris's mission to educate young Black Americans. Colson benefited from being born into a free family in Virginia, but he became part of a new system that quickly eroded the distinctions between those born free and those born to slavery.[3]

The story of the Colson family offers insight into how emancipation affected the experience of Virginians who were the descendants of free Black Americans. But it is important to note the effect of community and location on the lives of free Black people before the Civil War. Petersburg, Virginia, had a large free Black population during the early nineteenth century, making up almost 25 percent of the city's population of 8,322 in 1830. On the eve of the war, the free Black community numbered 3,164 compared to 5,680 enslaved people, and about 9,000 white residents. Many of Petersburg's free Black

Chimborazo School register, 1868–69, kept in Richmond by Elizabeth Cartland (1849–1936). *VMHC*

residents lived in Pocahontas, also known as Pocahontas Island, which was on the Appomattox River, and was a community exclusively of free people, some of whom made their living from the river as fishermen or boatmen. There is not much known about the first James Colson, but he appears in legal records in 1804 after purchasing land in Petersburg. His son William left extensive records of his business enterprises, including his partnership with Joseph Jenkins Roberts, another free Black Petersburg resident. Roberts, Colson, and Company shipped goods to and from the colony of Liberia, which the U.S. government created specifically to meet the goal of the American Colonization Society to relocate Black Americans to Africa. William Colson married Sarah Elebeck in 1826, the daughter of another of Petersburg's prominent free Black families, and they had three children together, including James Major Colson. William Colson died in Liberia in 1835, while his business partner, Roberts, became Liberia's first president after the colony gained independence in 1847. But William Colson had left his family a legacy that allowed his son, James Major Colson, and his grandson, James Major Colson, Jr., to establish themselves in a society that otherwise restricted their opportunities.[4]

The Colson family had advantages that allowed them to gain education, skills, and property within a system of white supremacy, where Black success was curtailed and the most common condition of Black Virginians was enslavement. This often meant that men like James Major Colson, Sr., had to work harder and cater to white clients to succeed. Colson earned a reputation as a skilled shoemaker purveying to wealthy Petersburgers, and he was able to continue his business during the Civil War, selling boots at a time when materials were scarce and inflation was high. Although being free gave the Colsons advantages that enslaved people did not have, emancipation leveled the playing field. The Freedmen's Bureau established schools, such as the Chimborazo School in Richmond, Virginia, alongside those founded by educated Black Americans,

DAILY SCHOOL REGISTER for *Chimborazo* School, in *Richmond* State of *Virginia*, for the month commencing *10th mo 8th*, 18*68*, and ending ____________, 18__, taught by *Bessie Cartland*

School No.	Names of Scholars.	Years of Age.	No. of Days Attendance.
1	Celia Braxton	9	18
2	Felicia A. Willis	10	18
3	Francis Bailer	10	18
4	Mary L. Washington	12	18
5	Mary Washington	9	18
6	Margret Johnson	12	16
7	Isabella Williams	12	18
8	Florence A. Jane	10	17
9	Susy A. Jefferson	7	18
10	Cornelia A. Lewis	10	18
11	Julia Jones	11	18
12	Mary Woolrich	15	5
13	Mary Louise Smith	14	18
14	Jetty W. Jackson	9	
15	Isaiah Scott	7	17
16	Thomas Williams	8	18
17	Robert Fountain	8	18
18	Daniel Williams	5	16
19	Albert Spencer	8	7
20	Daniel Vaughns	4	16
21	Rosy Bunbels	12	17
22	Emma Jane Willits	4	15
23	Lucy Williams	6	16
24	Susan Jane	11	16
25	Josephine Canda	20	17
26	Mazia Bell	15	12
27	Emily E. Blair	9	17
28	Mary E. Brown	10	12
29	Sallie Harris	5	5
30	Sarah Francis	8	15
31	Lizetta Johnson	9	15
32	Hester Johnson	15	15
33	Cely Johnson	10	15
34	Minerva Bell	10	13
35	Martha F. Williams	11	14
36	Nannie Eaton	10	14
37	Maria Burleigh	20	15
38	Francis E. Jefferson	29	12
39	Francis Brown	19	8
40	Mindora Cook	12	14
41	Stephen Baden	11	15
42	Daniel Webster	10	14
43	Tommy Gray	9	13
44	William H. Carter	12	15
45	Peter Brice	7	15
46	Jeffe Hood	6	13
47	Ann Annerson	13	12
48	Caroline Harris	7	10
49	Harriet Brooks	26	14
50	Sammy Christian	5	12
51	Robert B. Williams	7	12
52	Caleb Branch	8	12
53	David Paige	10	10
54	Charlie Davis	8	13
55	James Richardson	9	*
56	John Cane	10	12
57	Wilson Johnson	12	12
58	Thomas Johnson	8	11
59	Keziah Smith	14	10

QUESTIONS FOR TEACHERS.

(Answers to be given for the month.)

Name and location of your School? *Chimborazo*

Of what grade? *Primary*

When did your present session commence? *8th of 10th mo*

When is your present session to close? *In 5 mo.*

Is your school supported by any Educat'l Society? *No* and by what Society?

Is your School supported wholly by a local School Board? *No* Name.

Is your School supported *in part* by a local School Board? *No* Name.

Is your School supported wholly by the Freedmen? *No*

Is your School supported *in part* by the Freedmen? *No*

Have you had Bureau transportation this term? *Yes*

Who owns the school building? *The Bureau*

Is rent paid by Freedmen's Bureau? *Yes* and how much?

What number of Teachers and Assistants in your School? *One teacher*

Are they white or colored? *White*

Total enrollment for the month? *62*

Male? *22* Female? *40*

No. enrolled last report?

No. left School this month? *Not any*

No. new Scholars this month?

What is the average attendance? *46*

No. Pupils who pay tuition? *None*

No. white Pupils? *None*

No. always present? *31*

No. always punctual? *32*

No. over sixteen years of age? *8*

No. in Alphabet?

No. who spell and read easy lessons?

No. of advanced readers?

No. in Geography? *None*

No. in Arithmetic?

No. in higher branches? *None*

No. in Writing? *None*

No. in Needlework? *None*

No. free before the war?

Have you a Sabbath School? *No*

No. Teachers in Sabbath School?

No. Pupils in Sabbath School?

Have you an Industrial School? *No* No Pupils?

State kind of work done?

REMARKS.

I certify that the above are true and correct statistics

Teacher.

John Mitchell, Jr. (1863–1929), from *Negro Office-Holders in Virginia, 1865–1895*, by Luther P. Jackson (Norfolk, Va.: Guide Quality Press, 1945). *VMHC*

including the one that Fannie Meade Bolling started in Petersburg.[5]

Some of those who were born to freedom may have resented the loss of status, but many like Colson embraced the chance to provide uplift and opportunity for other Black Americans. Access to education and the emergence of a Black middle class led to the ascendancy of the "New Negro." Historian Henry Louis Gates, Jr., describes Black intellectuals' advocacy of "the New Negro" as a way to resist white supremacy through the adoption of white middle-class standards and a desire to use this status to elevate their race. In 1895, John Mitchell, Jr., editor of the Black newspaper *The Richmond Planet*, commented on this new eventuality by stating that "[t]he lowly and the illiterate do not specially desire to exercise the privileges, because they have neither money, the education nor the time to enjoy them, but there are others who do. We have a class of colored people, the 'New Negro' who have arisen since the war, with education, refinement and money." On a national level, this was in line with W. E. B. Du Bois's call for the creation of a "talented tenth," who would gain status and influence in order to fight discrimination and break racial barriers. Mitchell himself was born into slavery, but he attended a normal school in Richmond which prepared him to teach for a year before pursuing journalism.[6]

Not all of those who were free before slavery ended had the advantages of the Colson family, or the ability to elevate the status of those outside their family circle. Samuel Johnson was a free Black resident of Northern Virginia who worked as a blacksmith and purchased his wife and daughter. His daughter Lucy, whom he legally held in slavery to allow her to remain in the state, was able to obtain freedom after her father's death as indicated by his estate, and was able to purchase freedom for her husband, Sandy Elkins. Lucy died before slavery ended, and Sandy moved with their two sons, Jasper and Jerome, to Washington, D.C., where they established a successful blacksmithing and wheelwright business. Johnson's descendants worked in lower- and middle-class occupations, either renting homes or owning property while taking in boarders. Still, Johnson's descendants had a level of stability that other Black families would not have following emancipation. Indeed, Jasper's son, William C. Elkins, went to New York and became a musician, helping develop Black musical theater, including the 1903 show *In Dahomey*, the first musical written by Black Americans to be performed on Broadway. Samuel Johnson's family also calls to attention another important fact about free Black Virginians: for various reasons, they and their children did not always stay in the state. Freedom, especially after the end of the Civil War, meant mobility and often better opportunities that lay elsewhere. Additionally, in the case of Johnson's family, having marketing skills passed down from family members, as well as property, gave the descendants of free Black Virginians the foundations for success, if not the ability to create opportunities for others, as in Colson's case.[7]

Emancipation also promised to make Black Virginians equal to one another in the eyes of the law, though not equal to white Virginians. Regardless of previous status, Black people had a keen understanding of their potential political power, forged in the experience of interacting in labor gangs, marketplaces, and religious gatherings. These activities allowed relationships to form and important connections to be made, which would provide the basis for political awareness and organizing. Uniting through common experience and sharing faith and values during slavery, Black Virginians co-opted these existing networks to identify political leaders and spread information. Following emancipation, Black Virginians gathered in Richmond, Norfolk, and Alexandria to demand equal treatment, citizenship, and voting rights. Some Black men in Virginia even voted in local elections in 1865, although their ballots were disregarded. Instead, the Reconstruction policies of President Andrew Johnson intervened—allowing leniency for former Confederates running for office and participating in the state legislature. Much to the dismay of Black Virginians, some of the same men who had conducted the rebellion and waged war against the Union were now elected to the state government and to the U.S. Congress. Virginia's state legislature did not ratify the 14th Amendment, which would have recognized the citizenship of the formerly enslaved and prevented Confederate military officers and civil officials from holding office. Therefore, Republicans did not allow the newly elected senators and representatives from former Confederate states to take their seats in Congress. But in Virginia, the reactionaries were still able to make headway in reestablishing aspects of white supremacy, including a vagrancy law meant to reproduce the essence of enslavement. Any person deemed a "vagrant," or more specifically someone not agreeing to work for insufficient wages, would be forced to work for three months at the "best" wages possible. If the individual ran away from this forced contract, they would be made to work one additional month at no pay while wearing a ball and chain. This "false start" to reconstruction was remedied by the Reconstruction Act of 1867—a response to white supremacists' efforts to restrict Black freedom through discriminatory state laws and resistance to the 14th Amendment.[8]

Francis H. Pierpont (1814–1899), about 1864, carte-de-visite photograph. *Courtesy of Library of Virginia*

Republicans initiated sweeping Congressional legislation that divided the former Confederate states into military districts, reversed the efforts of the newly formed state legislatures, and called for the drafting of new state constitutions. Virginia Governor Francis H. Pierpont led a coalition of white and Black Republicans and former Whigs in an effort to write a new state constitution that would embrace the tenets of Congressional Reconstruction. In 1867, voters were able to participate in a referendum on whether to hold a constitutional convention, and Black male voters turned out in impressive numbers. In Augusta County, in the Shenandoah Valley, 1,024 Black men voted for the convention, while nine Black men voted against it. These voters represented 75 percent of the eligible Black voters in the county, while only about 33 percent of white residents voted to hold the convention in August, with the vast majority voting against it. The enthusiasm of Black voters was clear on the state level as well, when 88 percent of eligible Black voters exercised the franchise, while only around 63 percent of white Virginians went to the polls. Twenty-four Black men were among the sixty-eight Republicans elected to participate in the drafting of this new constitution, engaging in debates under the supportive gaze of Black men and women watching from the gallery.

More than half of the Black delegates had been free before the war, and most of them were literate. Article three of the proposed constitution outlined state election procedure and indicated that "Every male citizen of the United States, 21 years old, who shall have been a resident in this state 12 months . . . shall be entitled to vote upon all questions submitted to the people at such election." But Virginia, like other former Confederate states during Reconstruction, was the scene of political conflict between progressive elements of the Republican Party and conservatives in the Democratic Party, many of whom had played significant leadership roles in the Confederate government and military. Forward-thinking Republicans who embraced the realization of civil rights for Black Americans, dubbed "radical" by their opponents, wanted protection of Black male suffrage, free public schools, and revocation

"The State Convention at Richmond, Va., in Session," from *Frank Leslie's Illustrated Newspaper*, February 15, 1868. *Courtesy of the Library of Virginia*

of citizenship for former Confederates. However, conservatives opposed the state constitution and prevented its ratification. They objected to the removal of the voting rights of men who had held public office before the Civil War but participated in the Confederate government. Nonetheless, proponents of the new constitution agreed to vote on this issue in a separate referendum. The constitution passed, but conservatives were able to defeat disenfranchisement of former Confederates at the polls. The Underwood Constitution, as it became known, was finally ratified in July 1869.[9]

The creation of a new state government, and the ratification of the 14th and 15th Amendments to the U.S. Constitution, allowed Virginia's representatives to take their seats in Congress, and made possible the representation of Black Virginians at the state and local level for the first time. Political participation was a new experience for all Black men in Virginia, although those men who were born free were often in a better position to assume political leadership. Including the initial twenty-four Black members of the state constitutional convention, almost one hundred Black men won election to positions in the reconstituted state government. The "radical" wing of the Republican Party chose white politician and acting military governor Henry Horatio Wells as their candidate for the 1870 state election, paired with Joseph Dennis Harris, a member of a free Black North Carolina family who moved to Ohio in the 1850s. Harris was a physician who came to Virginia with the Union Army, eventually settling in the state and becoming involved in politics. Conservatives sided with moderate Republicans to win election for Gilbert C. Walker as governor, but the importance of Black political power had become

John C. Underwood (1809–1873), about 1865–80, glass plate. *Library of Congress*

First Baptist Church, Manchester, Va., from *Sermons on Several Occasions*, by Rev. A. Binga, Jr. ([Richmond, Va.,] 1889). *VMHC*

apparent, especially to white conservatives who were so concerned about the radicals' influence that they abandoned their own candidates to support Walker's relatively conservative "True Republican" ticket. The mere possibility of Wells later winning a seat in the Senate and Harris stepping up as governor chilled the blood of white supremacists, regardless of political party.[10]

The roots of Black political organization and influence reach well before emancipation, as both free and enslaved Virginians had already forged community connections that prepared them for voting and holding office. For example, the establishment of independent, Black-led churches was essential to both spiritual and political development during Reconstruction and long after. Most churches had a mix of white and Black congregants, although some Black congregations existed in urban areas before emancipation, but usually under the leadership of white clergy. In the years following the end of the Civil

War, the majority of Black Christians formed their own congregations—a historical turning point that was vital to the Black spiritual development. In Petersburg, Gillfield Baptist Church was established as an independent Black church after 1800, although all of the pastors were white, with one exception, until after emancipation. The members of the church included both free and enslaved people who were able to play limited roles in the church leadership, including choosing their own pastor on several occasions, although this still meant appointing white spiritual leaders. In 1865, Henry Williams, Jr., was appointed as pastor by the congregation after preaching at the church while passing through the city on his way to missionary service. Williams was born free in Virginia, but grew up in Ohio; he even took a short trip to Africa. He did not have a formal education, but after returning to Ohio he embraced the teachings of Christianity and became part of the Underground Railroad. Williams accepted the call to preach for the Gillfield Baptist Church, and also won election to the Petersburg Common Council in 1872. In this way, he accepted both spiritual leadership and civic responsibility, demonstrating that the two could be entwined. Although Williams only served one term, in the years following emancipation independent Black churches were essential to political organization, establishment of community, spiritual uplift, and hope for the future.[11]

By the 1870s, political challenges facing Black Americans went beyond protection of the right of men to vote, and became entwined with state politics and social matters. The political issue with the most lasting impact was conservative Democrats' insistence on paying back Virginia's massive prewar debt, at the expense of much-needed improvements to infrastructure, education, and medical care. During the 1870s, the Republican Party in Virginia became more focused on national issues and political maneuvering, and radicals became a minority in the party. White Republican leadership did not address the issues that most concerned Black voters, resulting in dissatisfaction among them and their representatives. Conservatives gained control of the legislature during this period and used their influence to centralize power, restrict voting, and redraw voting districts to disperse Black voting power, known as "gerrymandering." Voting restrictions did not directly target Black voters but disenfranchised anyone convicted of petit larceny, or punished them by whipping. Those most affected by this would be poor Virginians, both white

William Mahone (1826–1895), about 1865–80, glass plate. *Library of Congress*

and Black, but when combined with other efforts to discriminate against Black Americans it significantly weakened their political power.[12]

The most impactful conservative political measure, however, was the Funding Act of 1871, which pledged to repay around $37 million of debt incurred before the war. Although the act was supposed to allow the state to pay only two-thirds of its prewar debt, the actual result of the transactions caused tax revenue to fall below half of what was required to pay creditors and operate the state, including paying for public schools. Conservatives in control of the state legislature were unwilling to repudiate any state debt and unable to adjust the impact of the Funding Act by increasing income taxes and ending tax "coupons" for those who purchased state bonds. Conservatives considered paying the debt a matter of honor, as well as an act of defiance against the North. Admitting that the prewar debt was difficult to pay simply magnified the disappointment of the failed attempt at secession and independence. This unswerving commitment to pay the debt, regardless of effect, meant that there was little available tax revenue left for infrastructure, public education, hospitals, or other public works.

In response, a coalition of white and Black Republicans and Democrats formed under the leadership of former Confederate General William "Little Billy" Mahone to constitute the Readjuster Party. This party dedicated itself to "readjusting" the state debt by requesting a reduction in the debt and paying the remainder through long-term, low-interest bond sales. Essentially, the Readjusters admitted the debt was too much to pay off in total, and they saw more benefit to working with northern investors and focusing on the needs of the citizens of the Commonwealth, both white and Black. Known as one of few "fusion" parties formed during the Reconstruction era, it was actually a loosely associated voting bloc of urban Black and immigrant workers, Black farmers and farm laborers in eastern Virginia, and white farmers in the western part of the state. In this way, the party was not an alliance of Black and white voters in the true sense, but instead pockets of white or Black voters concerned about the Funder policies regarding public education and taxes, as well as the effect of the Funding Bill on the state budget and legislators' inability to improve infrastructure.[13]

The Readjuster leadership was predominately white, although much like the Republican Party during Congressional Reconstruction, there were

"Readjuster State Convention at Richmond," Walter Goater, from *Frank Leslie's Illustrated Newspaper*, June 25, 1881. *Courtesy of Library of Virginia*

opportunities for office-holding for Black men at the regional and local level. In 1879, the Readjusters gained control of the state legislature, followed by Mahone assuming a seat in Congress as a senator the next year, and Petersburg's William Cameron securing the governor's office for the party in 1881. These victories increased the state revenue from taxes and allowed for improvements in public schools and medical education. Without the concern for paying off the debt through bonds that involved tax "coupons" for investors, taxes could go to these worthy projects. Notably, all of this was done with the support of Black Virginians, many of whom felt neglected and underrepresented by the Republican Party. Black male voters were acutely aware of their political power, as evidenced by their organizing efforts, including a Black labor convention in Richmond in 1875 and an 1880 proposal for a "Colored State Convention," to be held in Petersburg.

Black voters had demonstrated their intention to garner political power to support whatever party would benefit them the most. White Readjusters understood the need to earn Black voters' support, evidenced by George W. Booker's strategic proposition to Mahone in 1881. Booker was a conservative Republican who represented Virginia in Congress from 1869 to 1871 and who served in the General Assembly. Although not a Readjuster and retired from politics, Booker proposed removing the connection between taxes and voting, and ending whipping as punishment for petit larceny, which was a deliberate holdover from slavery. Most importantly, Booker suggested regaining control over federal patronage, which would allow Mahone to reward supporters with government jobs, as well as state and local appointments. Mahone and the Readjusters were able to accomplish these things because of Mahone's ability to leverage his position in the Senate. Indeed, Readjuster rule greatly benefited Black Virginians by awarding many federal appointments in the Post Office, Treasury, and Pension Bureau in Virginia, along with the Department of the Interior. However, white Readjusters did monopolize the leadership positions in the party, and they were more concerned with gaining Black support than with combating the effects of white supremacy. Black Readjusters were rewarded with local appointments, and their reforms were particularly aimed at improvements that benefited both Black and white people, while not addressing the racism and discrimination that prevented Black Virginians from realizing political or financial independence.[14]

However, the success of the white Readjusters like Mahone and Cameron led to success for Black Readjusters as well, including Alfred Harris. Harris was elected to the House of Delegates in 1881 and served four terms, until 1888, representing Dinwiddie County and supported by both factions within the Republican Party. Harris became involved in Republican Party politics in the 1870s in Alexandria. He had a strong commitment to education and was married to a public school principal, Ida R. Morris. He introduced the bill that created the Virginia Normal and Collegiate Institute, consistent with the Readjusters' commitment to education and Harris's own dedication to Black achievement and opportunity. Normal schools were designed specifically to train teachers, and although Virginia did constitutionally require public education of Black and white children alike, the schools were segregated and trained Black teachers were needed for Black schools. Many schools with Black pupils had white teachers, something some Black Readjusters wished to remedy. The V.N.C.I. would join the Colver Institute (later known as Virginia Union University) and Hampton Normal and Agricultural School in providing this essential education to teachers, but the collegiate institute also would provide bachelor's degrees.[15]

Petersburg is an excellent example of how Black Virginians wielded the political power gained from association with the Readjuster Party to better their community. Though the V.N.C.I. stands as a prominent example of how Black Readjusters were able to achieve their goals of offering additional educational opportunities, it was part of a larger change for the community. Alfred Harris insisted that the V.N.C.I. have an all-Black Board of Visitors (with the exception of one white ex officio member), and that all faculty and staff be Black people. Additionally, the school offered eight-week teaching programs that would qualify individuals to teach in public schools. However, Black Readjusters faced a tougher battle in ensuring that there would be jobs for Black teachers, and that Black students would have teachers who had their best interests in mind. Although Mahone and other white Readjusters were unwilling to back the push to replace white teachers in Petersburg's segregated Black schools with Black educators, community leaders took it upon themselves to demand this change. This was done by actually supporting segregation through the argument that if schools were to be separated racially, then they should be completely so. By pointing out that to be truly segregated, Black students must be taught by Black teachers, more teaching positions would be open to Black educators, including those recently completing the normal school program at the V.N.C.I. Black residents of Petersburg were able to leverage their power with Governor Cameron, who dissolved the school board and replaced its members with those who would be willing to employ Black teachers.[16]

Though the victories of the Readjuster Party did result in improvements that unified Black Virginians regardless of their previous status or that of their parents, free or enslaved, this period of Black political influence was short-lived. Mahone's efforts to associate himself with the Republican Party disillusioned white Readjusters who had defected from the Democratic Party, and the level of Black participation led to white backlash against the Readjusters. Conservatives appealed to the racism and bigotry of some white Virginians who believed that the Readjuster movement had disrupted white supremacy, but it was what became known as the "Danville Riot" that brought an end to Readjuster rule. More properly described by historians as the "Danville Massacre," this conflict began on Saturday, November 3, 1883, when Charles Noel tripped over the foot of Hense Lawson, who was walking on the sidewalk with Davis Lewellyn. Though it was a seemingly simple altercation, the antecedents of the massacre were rooted in white control of public space and Black assertion of citizenship. Noel was white and Lawson and Lewellyn were Black men, and although Lawson offered an apology for accidentally tripping Noel, Lewellyn responded that Lawson did not need Noel's forgiveness, at which point Noel struck Lewellyn and a fight ensued, ending with Noel being bested and running away. This scuffle took place on the day the Democrats were holding a meeting in town to challenge the Readjuster Party, several days ahead of the 1883 election to be held that Tuesday. Noel went to the opera house where the Democrats had gathered, and enlisted two friends to go find Lawson and Lewellyn to exact revenge. The fight that followed between the two groups of men resulted in three police officers responding, one white and two Black, and a crowd of Black residents gathering. As the Black citizens demanded the arrest of a white man who had fired a pistol, more of the men in attendance at the meeting came out into the street and ordered the police officers to disperse the crowd. The standoff ended with many of the white Democrats drawing pistols and

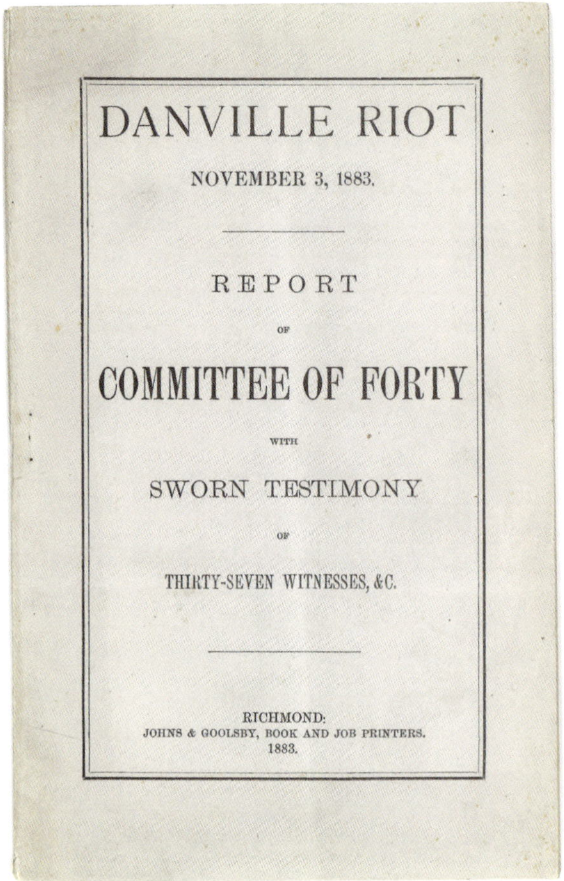
DANVILLE RIOT

NOVEMBER 3, 1883.

REPORT

OF

COMMITTEE OF FORTY

WITH

SWORN TESTIMONY

OF

THIRTY-SEVEN WITNESSES, &C.

RICHMOND:
JOHNS & GOOLSBY, BOOK AND JOB PRINTERS.
1883.

Danville Riot: Report of Committee of Forty with Sworn Testimony . . . (Richmond, 1883). *VMHC*

firing into the crowd of Black residents, resulting in the death of four Black men and a night of terror, when roaming groups of armed white men chased Black citizens from the street and patrolled the town. The news of the fighting in Danville spread fast and was used by the Democrats to fuel the already simmering racist opposition to the Readjusters by falsely claiming the "riot" was an uprising by Black Virginians encouraged by Mahone and his allies.[17]

The Democratic propaganda regarding the Danville Massacre strengthened the forces of white supremacy in Virginia and resulted in Democratic political victories, and thus began the decline of the Readjusters. Democrats set to work passing legislation to limit the power of the Black vote by giving Democrats control over precinct-level election judging, which would allow votes to be thrown out. In the 1885 governor's race, Fitzhugh Lee, former Confederate general and nephew of Robert E. Lee, co-opted Readjuster policies, including education and support for labor, while at the same time representing the return to white rule. Lee's victory, combined with Mahone's loss of his Senate seat the following year, ended the coalition forged by the Readjusters. Though Mahone and others continued to have influence in the Republican Party, the Democrats would control state politics for decades to come.[18]

Black political power was diminished but not totally defused, as evidenced by the career of John Mercer Langston. Langston was born free in Virginia, the son of a white enslaver and the enslaved woman he freed. Langston's parents lived together, but could not marry by law, and after their deaths in 1834, Langston moved to Ohio where he studied at the famed Oberlin College, earning his master's degree and going on to study law. He was an active abolitionist in the 1850s, and during the Civil War he was a recruiter for Black regiments, including the well-known 54th Massachusetts. Langston's involvement with the Freedmen's Bureau inspecting schools after the war brought him back to Virginia and led to administrative positions at Howard University, including president. After holding a diplomatic position to Haiti and the Dominican Republic, Langston was appointed president of the newly founded Virginia Normal and Collegiate Institute in January 1866 and remained in post until December 1867. Langston was extremely popular among students, but less so among the Democratically appointed white members of the school's Board of Visitors, which prompted Langston to resign and reenter politics. Langston's association with the Republican Party and his experience in

John Mercer Langston (1829–1897), about 1868–75, glass plate.
Library of Congress

education made him a strong candidate for the U.S. House of Representatives in 1888, although Mahone did not support Langston and the two had a tenuous relationship. Langston's base of power was in Petersburg, where there was enough support for the Republican candidate to make Langston a serious contender for a seat in the House. The Democratic candidate, Edward C. Venable, won the election. But Republican challenges to the results, based on suspicions of dishonesty and election interference on the part of conservatives, led to Venable being unseated and Langston assuming the office, although he only served from late September 1889 to early March 1890. However, at the same time that John Mercer Langston held the distinction of being the first Black man to serve as a representative to the U.S. Congress from Virginia, the state was slipping into what historians would call the "Jim Crow" era. It was the significant gains made by Black Virginians that led to white supremacist efforts to curtail Black political power.[19]

The victory for white supremacy in Virginia was cemented in 1902, when Democrats successfully passed a new state constitution—one that rolled back the gains made by Black Virginians and their allies since 1865. Virginia voters had defeated referenda to amend the Constitution in 1888, 1893, and 1897, but low voter turnout in 1900 allowed conservatives to call for the drafting of a new constitution. Although the Democrats made pretense about reducing corruption as the excuse for limiting Black suffrage, it was deep-seated concern over the power of the Black vote, particularly when combined with the rural white vote, that solidified the voting restrictions that would be embedded in the 1902 Constitution. The convention wished to subvert the 15th Amendment, which protected the voting rights of Black Americans, by including sections that created additional voter eligibility requirements. However, voting restrictions based on property holding, wealth, and literacy would also restrict the rights of working-class and poor whites, which in turn might lessen their support of the new constitution. The white politicians drafting the new constitution instead settled upon a set of restrictions that, although not overtly mentioning race, would secure white political supremacy. Men who had served in the Union or Confederate armies, or were the son of someone who had served, were automatically allowed to vote, but everyone else would need to pay a property tax of at least one dollar a year or prove he could read and explain a given section of the state constitution. These limitations would disenfranchise impoverished or illiterate white voters, except there was a temporary "understanding clause" that allowed illiterate voters to demonstrate they understood a given section that was read to them. The architect of these provisions, Democratic politician Carter Glass, admitted that the understanding clause could be administered discriminately, with simple clauses being read to white voters and more complex ones presented to Black voters. To compound this, voters had to pay a poll tax six months in advance of the election. In practice, these restrictions significantly impacted the number of white men who could vote as well, because the framers of the new constitution were predominately concerned with placing political power in the hands of white elites.

The new constitution had a devastating effect on voter participation in Black communities in Richmond, Petersburg, Norfolk, and other urban areas where Black political power had been concentrated, cutting the number of eligible voters by at least three quarters. Black Virginians would have felt this loss of influence in different ways. One such example was the discontinuation of the bachelor's degree program at the Virginia Normal and Collegiate Institute, which prompted the change in its name to Virginia Normal and Industrial Institute. Students sent a petition to the state legislature appealing for the retention of the collegiate program, pointing out that segregation required Black Americans to have their own educators and professionals, which could not happen without a college program beyond the normal school model. The students couched their request within the dictates of white supremacy. They were not asking for additional rights or reform, and they accepted the industrial training as a matter of course. Still, their petition was ignored. White board members were added to create the plan of vocational training to replace the collegiate program, along with agricultural education. With the 1902 Constitution in place, Democrats could now restrict Black education and independence without the concern for any repercussions at the polls. The process that historians call "redemption" was complete in Virginia, as white Democrats regained power, and twisted the legal and political system to ensure they would hold on to it.[20]

The long winding path of war and Reconstruction led to Jim Crow, although there were some achievements for Black Virginians along the way. Though free African Americans during the antebellum period faced limitations on their ability to control their own fate and that of their family members, the post-emancipation era—apart from a period when something like genuine democracy prevailed from the late 1860s through the early 1880s—posed similar challenges to realizing the hopes and dreams of freedom. The common denominator between these two halves of the nineteenth century was the prevalence of white supremacy in the United States, embraced by conservative and moderate white Americans in both political parties. Although those Black Virginians who descended from free-born families may have had some advantages directly following the Civil War that formerly enslaved people did not have, the efforts of Black Virginians to pursue education and effectively garner political power created opportunities for all Black Virginians. However, as long as racism and discrimination permeated the social, economic, and political life of the United States, true freedom would lie just beyond their grasp.

Afterword

When Jim Dyke, Tim Sullivan, and Alvin Schexnider approached the Virginia Museum of History & Culture (VMHC) about an exhibition focused on the lives of free Black Virginians, I knew that I, like many others, did not know enough about this important history. While free Black people lived in Virginia beginning in the 1600s, they were, in many ways, hidden in plain sight. But, as the scholars contributing to this book make clear, they significantly impacted and influenced the Commonwealth's culture, politics, economy, and legal system.

As the oldest cultural institution in the Commonwealth, and one of the first and most distinguished historical organizations in the country, the VMHC is committed to connecting people to America's past through the unparalleled story of Virginia. We strive to preserve and interpret every aspect of the Commonwealth's rich and complex history. The VMHC is especially dedicated to bringing to light the stories of long-overlooked Virginians: stories important to making our understanding of the past fuller and more meaningful.

The exhibition, *Un/Bound: Free Black Virginians, 1619–1865*, and this companion book represent a commitment to that goal. Both introduce us to a community of Virginians whose story has been largely untold. *Un/Bound* explores the struggles and triumphs of free Black Virginians, both their everyday lives and those dramatic moments that demanded extraordinary courage, fortitude, and resolve. Their experiences demonstrate how a people could persevere through exceptional hardship. Their stories are both heartrending and inspirational.

Un/Bound also demonstrates how the VMHC's vast collection of more than nine million items can be deployed in new and meaningful ways. Objects displayed in the exhibition—a letter sent home from Canada after a successful escape attempt, an autobiography written by a man who purchased his freedom, and even a needlepoint crafted by a girl who was born free—are profound testimonials to the humanity of those whose stories are revealed in the exhibition.

Ultimately, *Un/Bound* explores the meaning and value of freedom. It lays bare the ways in which full freedom and citizenship were withheld from thousands of Virginians for centuries. It is also a tribute to the strength and ingenuity that free Black Virginians displayed as they navigated the challenges of living in a world that considered them less than equal. *Un/Bound* is a powerful American story—an invitation to thoughtfully reflect on our nation's past and to use it, purposefully, to help shape a better future.

Jamie O. Bosket
President & CEO, Virginia Museum of History & Culture

Contributors

Melvin Patrick Ely is the William R. Kenan, Jr. Professor of Humanities and Professor of History at the College of William & Mary. He researches and teaches the history of Black Americans and of the South. Before joining William & Mary, he taught at Yale University, where he received both the Prize for Outstanding Scholarly Publication and Research and the Prize for Teaching Excellence, and he served as Fulbright Professor of American Studies at the Hebrew University of Jerusalem. Dr. Ely is the author of *The Adventures of Amos 'n' Andy: A Social History of an American Phenomenon* (1991) and *Israel on the Appomattox: A Southern Experiment in Black Freedom from the 1790s through the Civil War* (2004), winner of the Bancroft Prize, the Albert J. Beveridge Award, and the Library of Virginia Literary Award for Nonfiction.

Cassandra L. Newby-Alexander is Professor of History and Endowed Professor of Virginia Black History and Culture and emeritus director of the Joseph Jenkins Roberts Center for African Diaspora Studies at Norfolk State University. Her research and teaching focuses on the history of Black Americans in Virginia. Her books include *Voices from within the Veil: African Americans and the Experience of Democracy* (2008), co-edited with William H. Alexander and Charles H. Ford; *An African American History of the Civil War in Hampton Roads* (2010); *Hampton Roads: Remembering Our Schools* (2009), with Charles H. Ford and Jeffrey Littlejohn; and *Virginia Waterways and the Underground Railroad* (2017).

Stephen Rockenbach is Professor of History, Interim Chair, Department of Sociology and Criminal Justice, and Assistant Dean of CHSS for Student Affairs at Virginia State University. He researches and teaches about the American Civil War in the border regions, guerrillas, community studies, historical memory, and slavery and emancipation. Dr. Rockenbach's publications include several scholarly essays and the book, *War Upon Our Border: Two Ohio Valley Communities Navigate the Civil War* (2016).

Sabrina G. Watson is an instructor and a doctoral candidate in the Department of History and Philosophy at Virginia State University. Her doctoral research is focused on free Black women in Virginia during the antebellum period. She has developed history course curriculum for Early College Academy at J. Sargent Reynolds Community College. ECA is a dual enrollment program that works with City of Richmond high school students to earn high school and college credits.

Evanda S. Watts-Martinez is Director of Counseling Services and Assistant Professor of Education at Richard Bland College of William & Mary and Co-Chair of the college's Racial Justice & Equity Task Force. She is the author of *Students' Self-Determined Motivation, Emotional Intelligence, and Academic Persistence: An Examination of Second Year Students at a Public and a Private Historically Black University* (2015).

Endnotes

Chapter 1

1. On these freedom suits, see Edmund S. Morgan, *American Slavery, American Freedom: The Ordeal of Colonial Virginia* (New York: W. W. Norton & Company, 1975), 331; and T. H. Breen and Stephen Innes, *"Myne Owne Ground": Race and Freedom on Virginia's Eastern Shore, 1640–1676* (New York: Oxford University Press, 1980). A slave owned (or at least claimed) by a free Black man: Breen and Innes, *Myne Owne Ground*, 13–15. White indentured servants of a free Black man: Breen and Innes, *Myne Owne Ground*, 105; John H. Russell, *The Free Negro in Virginia, 1619–1865* (Baltimore, Md.: Johns Hopkins Press, 1913), 10–11.
2. See text of the law at "'An act concerning Servants and Slaves' (1705)," Virginia Humanities, *Encyclopedia Virginia*, https://encyclopediavirginia.org/primary-documents/an-act-concerning-servants-and-slaves-1705/ (accessed October 8, 2024).
3. Russell, *Free Negro in Virginia*, 40–41.
4. Fredrika Teute Schmidt and Barbara Ripel Wilhelm, "Early Proslavery Petitions in Virginia," *William and Mary Quarterly*, ser. 3, 30 (1973): 133–46. The law of 1691 did not absolutely prohibit manumissions, but it did require the removal from Virginia of anyone who might be manumitted. A law of 1723 addressing the same subject allowed no exceptions except for meritorious service as determined by the governor and his council.
5. See Andrew Levy, *The First Emancipator: The Forgotten Story of Robert Carter, the Founding Father Who Freed His Slaves* (New York: Random House, 2005).
6. Henry Wiencek, "George Washington and Slavery," *Encyclopedia Virginia*, https://encyclopediavirginia.org/entries/washington-george-and-slavery/ (accessed October 8, 2024); Melvin Patrick Ely, *Israel on the Appomattox: A Southern Experiment in Black Freedom from the 1790s through the Civil War* (New York: A. Knopf, 2004), chaps. 1 and 2.
7. Letter from George Washington to John Francis Mercer, September 9, 1786, *Founders Online*, National Archives, https://founders.archives.gov/documents/Washington/04-04-02-0232 (accessed November 11, 2024).
8. See Ely, *Israel on the Appomattox*, 251–52.
9. See C. M. M. Mertens, "'These Troublesome Times among Us Have Caused All the People of Colour to Procure Certificates of Their Freedom': Free Black Registration in the Upper South, 1790–1830s," draft dissertation chapter (Leiden University, Netherlands, 2024), esp. 16, 29–30, drawing in part on Viola Franziska Müller, *Escape to the City: Fugitive Slaves in the Antebellum Urban South* (Chapel Hill: University of North Carolina Press, 2022).
10. Russell, *Free Negro in Virginia*, 114–15.
11. Ely, *Israel on the Appomattox*, 328–32.
12. Those counties were Accomack, in which free Black people constituted 25.5 percent of the free population and nearly 40 percent of the Black population; Dinwiddie (22.5 percent and 22.5 percent, respectively); Nansemond (28 percent and 31 percent); Southampton (23.5 percent and 24 percent); and Westmoreland (25.4 percent and 24.4 percent) (see United States 1850 Census Aggregates).
13. Ely, *Israel on the Appomattox*, 66, 398–99, 453–54 (will of Anthony White, 1848 and 1850).
14. Ibid., 103–5, 335–36; Philip Bowman, Prince Edward County will book 8 (1842), 409 (quotations).
15. Melvin Patrick Ely, "Black Slaveholders," in Larry J. Griffin and Peggy G. Hargis, eds., *The New Encyclopedia of Southern Culture: Social Class* (Chapel Hill: University of North Carolina Press, 2012), 249.
16. Melvin Patrick Ely, "Richard and Judith Randolph, St. George Tucker, George Wythe, Syphax Brown, and Hercules White: Racial Equality and the Snares of Prejudice," in Alfred F. Young, Gary B. Nash, and Ray Raphael, eds., *Revolutionary Founders: Rebels, Radicals, and Reformers in the Making of the Nation* (New York: Alfred A. Knopf, 2011), 326, 328–29, 334–36.
17. Ely, *Israel on the Appomattox*, 198 (Tucker) and 197 (Col. James Madison [not the former US President] on "idleness").
18. *Farmers' Register* 4 (May 1836): 4.

19. American Colonization Society, Virginia branch, minutes, November 4, 1823–February 5, 1859, 31, Virginia Museum of History & Culture.

20. Ely, *Israel on the Appomattox*, 73–74.

21. Petition of John G. Joynes, December 31, 1834, Legislative Petitions, Accomack County. Historian Luther P. Jackson, citing only the Joynes petition, depicts this train of events as part of a nine-year popular "campaign" of "blatant . . . community lawlessness" to drive free Black people out of the state. The actual events were repugnant enough, but Jackson's characterization of the narrative does not accurately track the Joynes petition. For a fuller discussion of these events and a critique of Jackson's description of them, see Ely, *Israel on the Appomattox*, 609n2.

22. Patrick H. Breen, *The Land Shall Be Deluged in Blood: A New History of the Nat Turner Revolt* (New York: Oxford University Press, 2015), 101–3.

23. Exchange of letters among James [?] Davidson, John D. Macklin, and John Floyd, August 27–30, 1831 ("publick mind"); letters of John Thompson Kilby, September 16, 1831; John D. Macklin, August 30, 1831; Asa Dupuy, September 19, 1831; William Wilson, September 19, 1831; Benjamin Walker et al., October 13, 1831; and Drury A. Bacon, October 7, 1831, all in Executive Papers, Gov. Floyd, Library of Virginia.

24. Ely, *Israel on the Appomattox*, 179–82.

25. Ibid., 182–83; Mertens, "These Troublesome Times," 49–50.

26. Ely, *Israel on the Appomattox*, 386, 598 (notes 122 and 123).

27. Gregg D. Kimball, *American City, Southern Place: A Cultural History of Antebellum Richmond* (Athens: University of Georgia Press, 2000), 131–34.

28. Ely, *Israel on the Appomattox*, 112–15.

29. One example: T. O. Madden, Jr., and Ann L. Miller, *We Were Always Free: The Maddens of Culpeper County, Virginia: A 200-Year Family History* (New York: W. W. Norton & Company, 1992), 49–54.

30. Ely, *Israel on the Appomattox*, 41–42.

31. Ibid., 156.

32. Suzanne Lebsock, *The Free Women of Petersburg: Status and Culture in a Southern Town, 1784–1860* (New York: W. W. Norton & Company, 1984), chap. 4; Madden, *We Were Always Free*; Eva Sheppard Wolf, *Almost Free: A Story about Family and Race in Antebellum Virginia* (Athens: University of Georgia Press, 2012), 119 (quotation).

33. Thomas E. Buckley, S.J., "Unfixing Race: Class, Power, and Identity in an Interracial Family," *Virginia Magazine of History and Biography* 102 (1994): 349–80 (quotation, p. 364).

34. Ted Delaney and Phillip Wayne Rhodes, *Free Blacks of Lynchburg, Virginia, 1805–1865* (Lynchburg, Va.: Warwick House Publishing, 2001), 15 (quotation); J. Susanne Simmons, "The Intersection of the Freed Black and Slave Communities in Augusta County, Virginia," paper delivered at the Shenandoah Valley Regional Studies Seminar, James Madison University, March 15, 1996; Sherrie S. McLeroy and William R. McLeroy, *Strangers in Their Midst: The Free Black Population of Amherst County, Virginia* (Bowie, Md.: Heritage Books, 1993).

35. Ely, *Israel on the Appomattox*, 320–21.

36. Ibid., 316–17.

37. Ibid., 284–301.

38. Ibid., 310 ("frequently"); Kirt von Daacke, *Freedom Has a Face: Race, Identity, and Community in Jefferson's Virginia* (Charlottesville: University of Virginia Press, 2012), 8 (quotation).

39. For one interracial marriage that was formally recognized, see Ely, *Israel on the Appomattox*, 69–70; ibid., 133–34, 193–95; Joshua D. Rothman, *Notorious in the Neighborhood: Sex and Families across the Color Line in Virginia, 1787–1861* (Chapel Hill: University of North Carolina Press, 2003).

40. Ely, *Israel on the Appomattox*, 157.

41. Molly Moore will and exception, will book 4, 437–38 (1810/1813); *Maria et al. v. Moore*, County Court order book 16, 135 (March 1808), 604 (August 1810); District Court order book, 1805–31, 463–65 (April 1814), all in Prince Edward County Records, Library of Virginia.

42. Rodney D. Green, "Black Tobacco Factory Workers and Social Conflict in Antebellum Richmond: Were Slavery and Urban Industry Really Compatible?" *Slavery and Abolition* 8 (1987): 195–96.

43. Ted Maris-Wolf, *Family Bonds: Free Blacks and Re-enslavement Law in Antebellum Virginia* (Chapel Hill: University of North Carolina Press, 2015).

44. One example: a law requiring free Black people who sold agricultural goods to secure a statement from some

"respectable" white person attesting that the goods had not been stolen. See Prince Edward County Court order book 27, 297 (December 1858), Library of Virginia.

45. *Richmond Daily Dispatch*, January 26, 1853.

46. See J. Bankhead Magruder to George Deas, August 9, 1861, in U.S. War Department, *The War of the Rebellion: A Compilation of the Official Records of the Union and Confederate Armies* (Washington, D.C.: Government Printing Office, 1880–1901), ser. 1, vol. 4, 573.

47. Ely, *Israel on the Appomattox*, 403–4.

48. Ibid., 405.

Chapter 2

1. Brendan Wolfe, "Free Blacks in Colonial Virginia," Virginia Humanities, *Encyclopedia Virginia*, https://encyclopediavirginia.org/entries/free-blacks-in-colonial-virginia/ (accessed September 28, 2024).

2. "We and They in Colonial America," *Facing History & Ourselves*, https://www.facinghistory.org/resource-library/we-they-colonial-america (accessed September 12, 2024).

3. Wolfe, "Free Blacks in Colonial Virginia"; John H. Russell, *The Free Negro in Virginia, 1619–1865* (Baltimore, Md.: Johns Hopkins Press, 1913), 124; Judith Weisenfeld, "Religion in African American History," *Oxford Research Encyclopedia of American History*, March 2, 2015, https://oxfordre.com/americanhistory/view/10.1093/acrefore/9780199329175.001.0001/acrefore-9780199329175-e-24 (accessed September 14, 2024); John Hope Franklin, *From Slavery to Freedom: A History of Negro Americans* (1947; New York: Alfred A. Knopf, 1968), 164–67; Yonaia Robinson, "Elizabeth Key Grinstead (1630–1665)," *BlackPast.org*, July 14, 2016, https://www.blackpast.org/african-american-history/grinstead-elizabeth-key-1630/ (accessed September 10, 2024); "July 21, 1656: Elizabeth Key Wins Her Freedom," *Zinn Education Project*, https://www.zinnedproject.org/news/tdih/elizabeth-key-wins-freedom/ (accessed September 12, 2024); "We and They in Colonial America"; Jone Johnson Lewis, "Elizabeth Key and Her History-Changing Lawsuit," *ThoughtCo.*, https://www.thoughtco.com/elizabeth-key-history-of-american-slavery-3530408 (accessed October 2, 2024).

4. Malcolm Foley, "Endurance Produced by Suffering: The Black Church in America," *Logos*, https://www.logos.com/grow/the-black-church-in-america/ (accessed September 20, 2024).

5. Albert J. Raboteau, *Slave Religion: The "Invisible Institution" in the Antebellum South* (1978; New York: Oxford University Press, 2004), 31–32, 100; Alicestyne Turley, *The Gospel of Freedom: Black Evangelicals and the Underground Railroad* (Lexington: University Press of Kentucky, 2022), 12; Thomas S. Kidd, "The Great Awakening in Virginia," *Encyclopedia Virginia*, https://encyclopediavirginia.org/entries/great-awakening-in-virginia-the/ (accessed September 20, 2024); Joseph B. Earnest, Jr., "The Religious Development of the Negro in Virginia" (Ph.D. diss., University of Virginia, 1914), 40.

6. Turley, *Gospel of Freedom*, 11–17, 30; Charles Colcock Jones, *The Religious Instruction of the Negroes in the United States* (Savannah, Ga.: Thomas Purse, 1842), 39, 42–49.

7. Eric C. Lincoln and Lawrence H. Mamiya, *The Black Church in the African American Experience* (Durham, N.C.: Duke University Press, 1990), 5–9; Raboteau, *Slave Religion*, 77–81; E. Franklin Frazier, *The Negro Church in America* (New York: Schocken Books, 1963), 8–10; "The Church in the Southern Black Community," *Documenting the American South*, https://docsouth.edu/church/intro.html (accessed April 16, 2024).

8. Jason Oliver Evans, "A Brief History of the Black Church's Diversity, and Its Vital Role in American Political History," *The Conversation*, February 3, 2023, https://theconversation.com/a-brief-history-of-the-black-churchs-diversity-and-its-vital-role-in-american-political-history-197511 (accessed October 2, 2024); Weisenfeld, "Religion in African American History"; Milton C. Sernett, ed., *African American Religious History: A Documentary Witness* (Durham, N.C.: Duke University Press, 1999), 54–68; Peter Randolph, *Sketches of Slave Life: Or, Illustrations of the "Peculiar Institution"* (Boston: n.p., 1855), 68.

9. Mark Galli, "The Inconceivable Start of African-American Christianity: Why Slaves Adopted Their Oppressor's Religion—and Transformed It," *Christianity Today*, February 21, 2014, https://www.christianitytoday.com/2014/02/inconceivable-start-of-african-american-christianity/ (accessed October 2, 2024); Lincoln and Mamiya, *Black Church*, 29; Lewis M. Purifoy, "The Southern Methodist Church and the Proslavery Argument," *Journal of Southern History* 32 (1966): 325; James W. C. Pennington, *The Fugitive Blacksmith; or, Events in the History of James W. C. Pennington*

"The Southern Methodist Church and the Proslavery Argument," *Journal of Southern History* 32 (1966): 325; James W. C. Pennington, *The Fugitive Blacksmith; or, Events in the History of James W. C. Pennington* (1850; Westport, Conn.: Negro Universities Press, 1971), 43–44.

10. Raboteau, *Slave Religion*, 145–57; Ava Chamberlain, "Self-Deception as a Theological Problem in Jonathan Edwards's 'Treatise Concerning Religious Affections,'" *Church History* 63 (1994): 541; Christine Leigh Heyrman, "The First Great Awakening," Divining America, *TeacherServe*, National Humanities Center, https://nationalhumanitiescenter.org/tserve/eighteen/ekeyinfo/grawaken.htm (accessed September 17, 2024); History.com Editors, "Great Awakening," *History.com*, August 6, 2024, https//www.history.com/topics/European-history/great-awakening (accessed September 21, 2024).

11. "First Baptist Church—Petersburg," *First Baptist Church*, https://thefirstbaptistchurchpetersburg.org (accessed March 5, 2024); Carol Ann Dennis, "First Baptist Church, Petersburg, Virginia (1756–)," *BlackPast.org*, March 5, 2014, https://www.blackpast.org/african-american-history/first-baptist-church-petersburg-virginia-1774/ (accessed September 10, 2024); "The Historic First Baptist Church, Organized in 1776," *The Historic First Baptist Church*, https://firstbaptistchurch1776.org (accessed March 6, 2024).

12. James H. Cone, ed., *A Black Theology of Liberation* (1970; Maryknoll, N.Y.: Orbis Books, 1993), 55–67; Raboteau, *Slave Religion*, 11; Leonard Lovett, "Aspects of the Spiritual Legacy of the Church of God in Christ: Ecumenical Implications," in David T. Shannon and Gayraud S. Wilmore, eds., *Black Witness to the Apostolic Faith* (Grand Rapids, Mich.: W. B. Eerdmans Pub. Co., 1985), 45–49; Dennis, "First Baptist Church."

13. Alejandro de la Fuente and Ariela J. Gross, *Becoming Free, Becoming Black: Race, Freedom, and Law in Cuba, Virginia, and Louisiana* (New York: Cambridge University Press, 2020), 56.

14. John Henderson Russell, "The Free Negro in Virginia: 1619–1865" (Ph.D. diss., Johns Hopkins University, 1913), 124.

15. Ibid., 125–26, 131; Fuente and Gross, *Becoming Free*, 41.

16. Thabiti Anyabwile, "Jonathan Edwards, Slavery, and the Theology of African Americans," *The Gospel Coalition*, https://media.thegospelcoalition.org/static-blogs/justin-taylor/files/2012/02/Thabiti-Jonathan-Edwards-slavery-and-theological-appropriation.pdf (accessed April 4, 2024).

17. Turley, *Gospel of Freedom*, 19–20; Ed Crews, "Peopling the Past: Meet Gowan Pamphlet," *Colonial Williamsburg*, https://research.colonialwilliamsburg.org/Foundation/journal/autumn12/pamphlet.cfm (accessed October 2, 2024); Lovett, "Aspects of the Spiritual Legacy," 45.

18. James H. Cone, "God and Black Suffering: Calling the Oppressors to Account," *Anglican Theological Review* 90 (2008): 701–12.

19. Rom. 6:15–23 (NIV); Timothy Robert Cochrell, "Foundations for a Biblical Model of Servant Leadership in the Slave Imagery of Luke-Acts" (Ph.D. diss., Southern Baptist Theological Seminary, 2015), 52; Gen. 1:26–27 (NIV); Crews, "Meet Gowan Pamphlet"; J. Nailah Avery, "White Jesus is Grounded in Colonialism. Black Jesus is Rooted in Liberation," *Broadview*, March 17, 2021, https://broadview.org/black-jesus-colonialism/#:~:text=Black%%20Jesus%20is%rooted%20in%20liberation (accessed September 22, 2024).

20. Takatso A. Mofokeng, "The Crucified among the Crossbearers: Towards a Black Christology" (Ph.D. diss., Protestant Theological University, 1983), 39.

21. Paul J. Wadell, "Fullness of Life: Hebrews 4:12–16; Mark 10:17–31," *The Christian Century*, October 6, 2009, https://www.christiancentury.org/article/2009-10/fullness-life (accessed October 2, 2024); "The Meaning of the Beatitudes: Jesus Christ's Beatitudes Explained," *ChristianPure*, http://christianpure.com/learn/beatitudes-explained?# (accessed April 17, 2024); Mat. 5:3–5, 11 (NIV); La Roy Sunderland, *The Testimony of God Against Slavery: Or A Collection of Passages from the Bible, which Show the Sin of Holding Property in Man* (Boston: Webster & Southard, 1835), 9.

22. Michael Card, *A Better Freedom: Finding Life as Slaves of Christ* (Downers Grove, Ill.: InterVarsity Press, 2009), 11, 74; George Bourne, *Picture of Slavery in the United States of America* (Middletown, Conn.: E. Hunt, 1834), 47.

23. Sernett, ed., *African American Religious History*, 64–68; Demetrius K. Williams, *The Cross of Christ in African American Christian Religious Experience: Piety, Politics, and Protest* (Lanham, Md.: Lexington Books, 2023), 34; James H. Cone, *The Cross and the Lynching Tree* (Maryknoll, N.Y.: Orbis Books, 2011), 18–27.

24. J. Deotis Roberts, "The Holy Spirit and Liberation: A Black Perspective," in Shannon and Wilmore, eds., *Black Witness to the Apostolic Faith*, 60; Wayne E. Croft, Sr., *A History of the Black Baptist Church: I Don't Feel No Ways Tired* (Valley Forge, Pa.: Judson Press, 2020), 1.

25. Tamica Jean-Charles, "For These Black Churches, Serving Their Community Was the Goal from the Start," *The Progress-Index*, July 1, 2021, https://www.progress-index.com/story/news/2021/07/01/gillfield-first-baptist-churches-played-part-integral-black-history-petersburg-virginia-slavery/7810268002/ (accessed September 22, 2024).

26. William E. Montgomery, "African American Churches in Virginia (1865–1900)," *Encyclopedia Virginia*, https://encyclopediavirginia.org/entries/african-american-churches-in-virginia-1865-1900 (accessed October 3, 2024).

27. Ibid.

28. "Remaking Virginia: Transformation Through Emancipation," Library of Virginia, *Virginia Memory*, https://www.virginiamemory.com/online-exhibitions/exhibits/show/remaking-virginia/church (accessed May 21, 2024); Gayraud S. Wilmore, *Black Religion and Black Radicalism: An Examination of the Black Experience in Religion* (New York: Doubleday & Co., 1973), 121.

29. Ibid.

30. Diana Kristine Durham, "Mary Smith Kelsey Peake (1823–1862)," Library of Virginia, *Dictionary of Virginia Biography*, http://www.lva.virginia.gove/public/dvb/bio.asp?b=Peake_Mary (accessed May 26, 2024).

31. Ibid.; "Mary Peake and the Emancipation Oak," *Melanin Mindscape*, September 17, 2019, https://melaninmindscape.com/mary-peake-and-the-emancipation-oak (accessed May 31, 2024).

32. Harvey Cox, *God's Revolution and Man's Responsibility* (Valley Forge, N.Y.: Judson Press, 1965), 99.

Chapter 3

1. Luther Porter Jackson, "The Virginia Free Negro Farmer and Property Owner, 1830–1860," *The Journal of Negro History* 24 (1939): 392–93.

2. Peter Kolchin, *American Slavery, 1619–1877* (New York: Hill and Wang, 1993), 81. Although statistics on free Black people before the Revolution are lacking, it is clear there were few in the population; as late as 1785, only about 1,800 out of 220,582 Black Virginians—less than one percent—were free. Between 1780 and 1810, however, the number of free Black people in Virginia surged, reaching 12,766 (4.2 percent) in 1790 and 30,570 (7.2 percent) by 1810. Research on Gabriel's actions by historians has revealed that the so-called rebellion was no more than a conspiracy. Books that cover this topic include Michael L. Nicholls's *Whispers of Rebellion: Narrating Gabriel's Conspiracy* (Charlottesville: University of Virginia Press, 2013). His book closely examines historical documents regarding the plot and who was encouraged to help with planning a rebellion. The book also discusses how other political and religious rhetoric may not have been an impetus for the plot. There are a number of historians who provide a summary of the events that took place in Haiti and their impact on plantation owners and enslaved African Americans. One such example is Martin Munro and Elizabeth Walcott-Hackshaw's *Reinterpreting the Haitian Revolution and Its Cultural Aftershocks* (Mona, Kingston: University of the West Indies Press, 2006). The history of Nat Turner's Rebellion comes from archival documents surrounding the event and confessions of the enslaved and free Black people who participated in the revolt, including Turner himself. The earliest history comes from Thomas R. Gray, who published *The Confessions of Nat Turner* in 1831. Another work that examines Nat Turner's Rebellion is Patrick H. Breen's *The Land Shall Be Deluged in Blood: A New History of the Nat Turner Revolt* (New York: Oxford University Press, 2016). Breen's study provides an interpretation of Gray's account of the confessions of Nat Turner and the co-conspirators. Breen challenges the historical evidence and provides his own analysis, which considers how white supremacy helped to maintain slavery and the reaction by the enslaved and free to the rebellion.

3. "Negro womens children to serve according to the condition of the mother (1662)," Virginia Humanities, *Encyclopedia Virginia*, https://encyclopediavirginia.org/primary-documents/negro-womens-children-to-serve-according-to-the-condition-of-the-mother-1662/ (accessed October 25, 2024); PBS, *Africans in America*, "Proclamation of Earl of Dunmore," https://www.pbs.org/wgbh/aia/part2/2h42t.html (accessed October 25, 2024); Woody Holton, *Forced Founders: Indians, Debtors, Slaves, and the Making of the American Revolution in Virginia* (Chapel Hill: University of North Carolina Press, 1999), 156; Ira Berlin, *Slaves Without Masters: The Free Negro in the Antebellum South* (New York: The New Press, 2007), 90.

4. "An ACT to amend the several laws concerning slaves (1806)," *Encyclopedia Virginia*, https://encyclopediavirginia.org/primary-documents/an-act-to-amend-the-several-laws-concerning-slaves-1806/ (accessed October 25, 2024).
5. Berlin, *Slaves Without Masters*, 94.
6. Ibid., 89; Nicholls, *Whispers of Rebellion*, 118; "An Act to amend the act concerning slaves, free negroes and mulattoes (April 7, 1831)," *Encyclopedia Virginia*, https://encyclopediavirginia.org/primary-documents/an-act-to-amend-the-act-concerning-slaves-free-negroes-and-mulattoes-april-7-1831/ (accessed October 25, 2024).
7. Ellen Eslinger, "Free Black Residency in Two Antebellum Virginia Counties: How the Laws Functioned," *The Journal of Southern History* 79 (2013): 261–98.
8. Berlin, *Slaves Without Masters*, 147.
9. "An Act to amend the act concerning slaves, free negroes and mulattoes (April 7, 1831)."
10. Jackson, "Virginia Free Negro Farmer," 391; Vanessa M. Holden, *Surviving Southampton: African American Women and Resistance in Nat Turner's Community* (Champaign: University of Illinois Press, 2021), 41.
11. Joe Watson, Commonwealth Cause, 1830, *Virginia Untold: The African American Narrative Digital Collection*, Library of Virginia, Richmond, Va. (cited hereafter as *Virginia Untold*), https://rosetta.virginiamemory.com/delivery/DeliveryManagerServlet?dps_pid=IE150096 (accessed October 25, 2024).
12. Ibid.
13. Holden, *Surviving Southampton*, 41.
14. Esther Evans, Commonwealth Cause, 1851, *Virginia Untold*, https://rosetta.virginiamemory.com/delivery/DeliveryManagerServlet?dps_pid=IE153217 (accessed October 25, 2024).
15. Harry Tunnell, Commonwealth Cause, 1851, *Virginia Untold*, https://rosetta.virginiamemory.com/delivery/DeliveryManagerServlet?dps_pid=IE152537 (accessed October 25, 2024).
16. "The African-American Experience in Isle of Wight County," *Isle of Wight County Museum*, https://www.historicisleofwight.com/the-african-american-experience-in-isle-of-wight-county.html (accessed October 25, 2024).
17. Eliza Harris, Free Negro Affidavit, 1807, *Virginia Untold*, https://rosetta.virginiamemory.com/delivery/DeliveryManagerServlet?dps_pid=IE1413983 (accessed December 2, 2024); Lizzy Harris (alias Eliza Harris), Commonwealth Cause, 1839, *Virginia Untold*, https://rosetta.virginiamemory.com/delivery/DeliveryManagerServlet?dps_pid=IE3518373 (accessed December 2, 2024); Jack (alias Jack Harden), Commonwealth Cause, 1825, *Virginia Untold*, https://rosetta.virginiamemory.com/delivery/DeliveryManagerServlet?dps_pid=IE3516613 (accessed October 25, 2024).
18. Berlin, *Slaves Without Masters*, 93; Holden, *Surviving Southampton*, 42.

Chapter 4

1. Tommy L. Bogger, *Free Blacks in Norfolk, Virginia, 1790–1860: The Darker Side of Freedom* (Charlottesville: University Press of Virginia, 1997), 37, 115; "Ship *Harriet*, Jan 1829," Subject File, 1792–1964, American Colonization Society Records, Manuscript Division, Library of Congress, Washington, D.C.
2. Marie Tyler-McGraw, *An African Republic: Black and White Virginians in the Making of Liberia* (Chapel Hill: University of North Carolina Press, 2007), 5–6.
3. Ibid., 3–4, 6.
4. June Purcell Guild, *Black Laws of Virginia: A Summary of the Legislative Acts of Virginia Concerning Negroes from Earliest Times to the Present* (Richmond, Va.: Whittet and Shepperson, 1936), 94–95; James Ciment, *Another America: The Story of Liberia and the Former Slaves Who Ruled It* (New York: Hill and Wang, 2013), 8.
5. Edward E. Baptist, *The Half Has Never Been Told: Slavery and the Making of American Capitalism* (New York: Basic Books, 2016), xxiii–xxv.
6. Bogger, *Free Blacks in Norfolk*, 11, 25–26, 29; Thomas C. Parramore, *Norfolk: The First Four Centuries* (Charlottesville: University Press of Virginia, 1994), 126–27.
7. Parramore, *Norfolk*, 127–28.
8. Ibid., 126; Izzy Gonzalez, "Religious History of Colonial Williamsburg," *StoryMaps*, April 10, 2021, https://storymaps.arcgis.com/stories/d241f1568a8f4a099e9191bc34ddbbec (accessed October 17, 2024); Thomas S. Kidd, "The Great Awakening in Virginia," Virginia Humanities,

Encyclopedia Virginia, https://encyclopediavirginia.org/entries/great-awakening-in-virginia-the/ (accessed October 17, 2024); William E. Montgomery, "African American Churches in Virginia (1865–1900)," *Encyclopedia Virginia*, https://encyclopediavirginia.org/entries/african-american-churches-in-virginia-1865-1900 (accessed October 18, 2024); Cassandra Newby-Alexander, Mae Breckenridge-Haywood, and the African American Historical Society of Portsmouth, *Black America Series: Portsmouth, Virginia* (Charleston, S.C.: Arcadia Publishing, 2003), 9, 13.

9. Charles River Editors, *The Colonization and Establishment of Liberia: The History of the West African Nation Before the Liberian Civil Wars* (Middleton, Del.: Charles River Editors, 2024), 4, 6.

10. Parramore, *Norfolk*, 126; J. Gus Liebenow, *Liberia: The Quest for Democracy* (Bloomington: Indiana University Press, 1987), 12–13.

11. Tyler-McGraw, *An African Republic*, 24, 26; Ciment, *Another America*, 8–10.

12. Bogger, *Free Blacks in Norfolk*, 44–45.

13. Robert Earle Anderson, *Liberia: America's African Friend* (Westport, Conn.: Greenwood Press, 1976), 6–66.

14. Harold D. Nelson, ed., *Liberia: A Country Study*, 3rd Edition (Washington, D.C.: U.S. Government Printing, 1985), 10.

15. Ibid.

16. Ibid.; Ray Cavanaugh, "Two Hundred Years Later, a Long-lost Document Sheds Light on the Purchase of Liberia," *The Washington Post*, November 20, 2021. The Duker Contract document can be found in the Bushrod Washington papers at the archives of the Chicago History Museum.

17. Nelson, ed., *Liberia*, 1; Liebenow, *Liberia*, 15–16; Anderson, *Liberia*, 68–69.

18. Nelson, ed., *Liberia*, 15–16.

19. Bogger, *Free Blacks in Norfolk*, 38.

20. Ibid., 38.

21. Ibid., 8–9, 28–30.

22. Ibid., 14, 33–34, 37; Parramore, *Norfolk*, 162–63.

23. Marie Tyler-McGraw, "Roberts Family," *Virginia Emigrants to Liberia*, May 1, 2008, https://virginians-to-liberia.iath.virginia.edu/research/roberts_family (accessed October 17, 2024); Tyler-McGraw, *An African Republic*, 76–77, 136.

24. Tyler-McGraw, *An African Republic*, 153–55.

25. Anderson, *Liberia*, 61.

26. Nelson, ed., *Liberia*, xxiii.

27. Ibid., xiv. Some historians have sought to divide the local groups into four categories: the Mande-tan (which included the Vai), the Mande-fu (composed of ten distinct groups, including the Mende, Gbande, Gbunde, Belle, Buzi or Loma, Kpelle, Mano, Geh, Gio, and Kra), the West Atlantic (which included the Gola and Kisi), and the Kru (composed of nine distinct groups, including the Kru, Bassa, Greo, Padebo or Half-Grebo, Sikon or Bush Bassa, Sapa, Tchien, Pudu, and a Teni) (ibid., 3; Anderson, *Liberia*, 9–11, 13–14; Tyler-McGraw, *An African Republic*, 7).

28. Nelson, ed., *Liberia*, xxiv.

29. Anderson, *Liberia*, 15, 17; Nelson, ed., *Liberia*, 16.

30. Nelson, ed., *Liberia*, 22–23.

31. Tyler-McGraw, *An African Republic*, 154–55.

32. Nelson, ed., *Liberia*, 17.

33. Anderson, *Liberia*, 79, 81.

34. Ibid., 80–81.

35. Liebenow, *Liberia*, 16–17.

36. Anderson, *Liberia*, 81–84.

37. Ciment, *Another America*, 3, 5; William Burke to Ralph R. Gurley, July 26, 1858, American Colonization Society Papers, Manuscript Division, Library of Congress.

Chapter 5

1. Edgar Toppin, *Loyal Sons and Daughters: Virginia State University 1882–1992* (Norfolk, Va.: Pictorial Heritage Pub. Co., 1992), 13–15; James Major Colson to Alfred Harris, April 21, 1883, Virginia State University Special Collections and Archives, Petersburg, Va.

2. Toppin, *Loyal Sons and Daughters*, 19–22; James Major Colson to Maj. Branch, May 6, 1883, Virginia State University Special Collections and Archives; J. J. Roberts and Sarah H. Colson, "The Colson Family," *The Negro History Bulletin* 10 (1946): 3–9, 20–21.

3. Toppin, *Loyal Sons and Daughters*, 13–17; Roberts and Colson, "The Colson Family," 6–7; Luther P. Jackson,

"Free Negroes of Petersburg, Virginia," *The Journal of Negro History* 12 (1928): 337–38.

4. Jackson, "Free Negroes of Petersburg," 366, 372; Roberts and Colson, "The Colson Family," 1–4; James Major Colson, Jr., is also referred to as James Major Colson III in family records. This depends on whether the James Colson born in 1784 is considered the "first" James Major Colson or not. In the records of Virginia State University, James Major Colson, Jr., is used as opposed to James Major Colson III, and that is the identifier used throughout this essay.

5. Jackson, "Free Negroes of Petersburg," 377; Roberts and Colson, "The Colson Family," 5–7; "The Freedmen's Bureau School at Chimborazo," *Church Hill People's News*, March 12, 2015, https://chpn.net/2015/03/12/the-freedmens-bureau-school-at-chimborazo/ (accessed October 22, 2024).

6. Henry Louis Gates, Jr., *Stony the Road: Reconstruction, White Supremacy, and the Rise of Jim Crow* (New York: Penguin Press, 2019), 190–92; "New York and Civil Rights," *The Richmond Planet*, June 29, 1895, 2 (quotation).

7. Eva Sheppard Wolf, *Almost Free: A Story About Family and Race in Antebellum Virginia* (Athens: University of Georgia Press, 2012), afterword, passim.

8. Jane Dailey, *Before Jim Crow: The Politics of Race in Postemancipation Virginia* (Chapel Hill: University of North Carolina Press, 2000), 15–17; Emily J. Salmon and Edward D. C. Campbell, Jr., eds., *The Hornbook of Virginia History* (Richmond: Library of Virginia, 1994), 50–53; Brent Tarter, "Vagrancy Act of 1866," Virginia Humanities, *Encyclopedia Virginia*, https://encyclopediavirginia.org/entries/vagrancy-act-of-1866/ (accessed October 21, 2024).

9. Virginia Constitutional Convention, *The Constitution of Virginia: Framed by the Convention which Met in Richmond, Virginia, on Tuesday, December 3, 1867, Passed April 17, 1868* (Richmond, 1868); Dailey, *Before Jim Crow*, 18–21; Edward L. Ayers, *The Thin Light of Freedom: The Civil War and Emancipation in the Heart of America* (New York: W. W. Norton & Company, 2017), 436–37, 444–45.

10. Richard Peters, George Minot, and George P. Sanger, eds., *The Statutes at Large and Proclamations of the United States of America, from December 1869 to March 1871 . . .* (39 vols.; Boston: Little, Brown, and Company, 1854-1901), 16:62; Constance E. H. Daniel, "Two North Carolina Families—The Harrises and the Richardsons," *Negro History Bulletin* 13 (1949): 3–23; Emily J. Salmon, "J. D. Harris (ca. 1833–1884)," *Encyclopedia Virginia*, https://encyclopediavirginia.org/entries/harris-j-d-ca-1833-1884/ (accessed October 21, 2024).

11. William H. Johnson, *A Sketch of the Life of Rev. Henry Williams, D.D., Late Pastor of the Gilfield [sic] Baptist Church, Petersburg, Virginia, with Ceremonies Incident to His Death, and to the Erection of a Monument to His Memory* (Petersburg, Va.: Fenn & Owen, 1901), 5–6; Nicole Myers Turner, *Soul Liberty: The Evolution of Black Religious Politics in Postemancipation Virginia* (Chapel Hill: University of North Carolina Press, 2020), chap. 1, passim.

12. Dailey, *Before Jim Crow*, 36–37.

13. Steven Hahn, *A Nation Under Our Feet: Black Political Struggles in the Rural South from Slavery to the Great Migration* (Cambridge, Mass.: The Belknap Press of Harvard University Press, 2003), 374–77; Salmon and Campbell, eds., *Hornbook of Virginia History*, 57–58.

14. Hahn, *A Nation Under Our Feet*, 409–11; Dailey, *Before Jim Crow*, 52–67.

15. Salmon and Campbell, eds., *Hornbook of Virginia History*, 58–59; Dailey, *Before Jim Crow*, 67–69.

16. Dailey, *Before Jim Crow*, 72–75.

17. Jane Dailey, "Deference and Violence in the Postbellum Urban South: Manners and Massacres in Danville, Virginia," *The Journal of Southern History* 63 (1997): 556–82.

18. Dailey, *Before Jim Crow*, 157–60; Salmon and Campbell, eds., *Hornbook of Virginia History*, 59–61.

19. William F. Cheek, "A Negro Runs for Congress," *The Journal of Negro History* 52 (1967): 14–34; Luis-Alejandro Dinnella-Borrego, "John Mercer Langston (1829–1897)," *Encyclopedia Virginia*, https://encyclopediavirginia.org/entries/langston-john-mercer-1829-1897/ (accessed October 21, 2024); Dailey, *Before Jim Crow*, 158–59; Hahn, *A Nation Under Our Feet*, 408–9.

20. Dailey, *Before Jim Crow*, 162–68; Toppin, *Loyal Sons and Daughters*, 54–55.

Index

Page numbers in *italics* refer to the illustrations